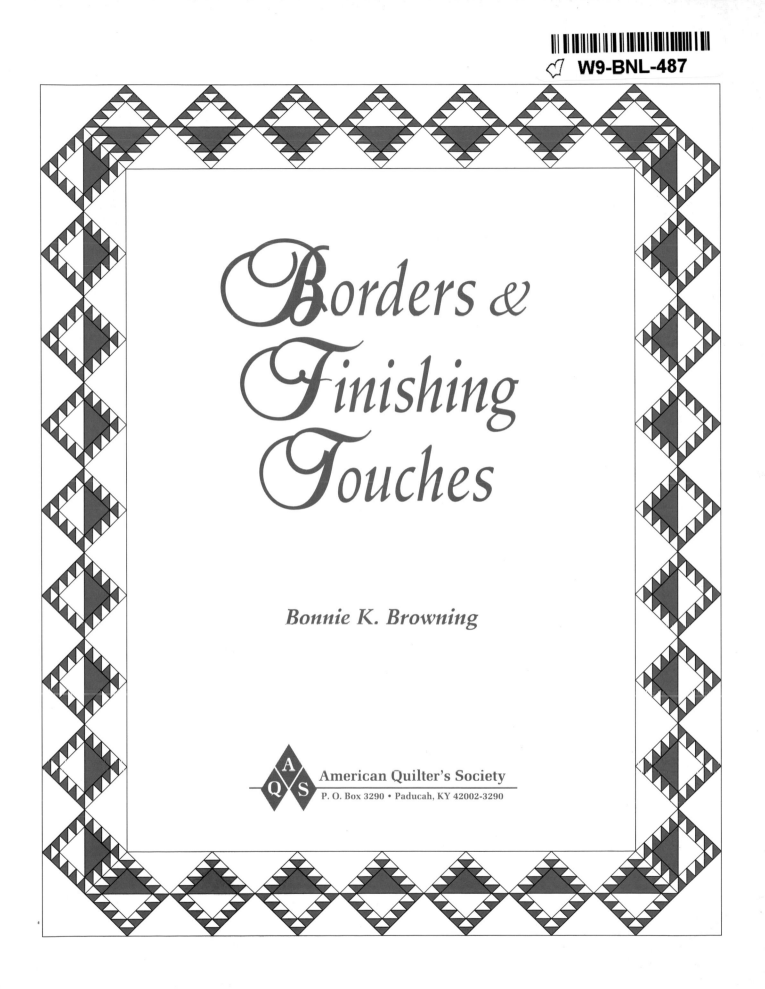

Borders & Finishing Touches

Bonnie K. Browning

American Quilter's Society
P. O. Box 3290 • Paducah, KY 42002-3290

Located in Paducah, Kentucky, the American Quilter's Society (AQS), is dedicated to promoting the accomplishments of today's quilters. Through its publications and events, AQS strives to honor today's quiltmakers and their work — and inspire future creativity and innovation in quiltmaking.

BOOK DESIGN/ILLUSTRATIONS: LANETTE BALLARD
COVER DESIGN: TERRY WILLIAMS & ANGELA SCHADE
PHOTOGRAPHY: CHARLES R. LYNCH & RICHARD WALKER

Library of Congress Cataloging-in-Publication Data
Browning, Bonnie, 1944-
      Borders & finishing touches / by Bonnie K. Browning.
         p.   cm.
      Includes bibliographical references.
      ISBN 0-89145-899-9
      1. Quilting. 2. Borders, Ornamental (Decorative arts)   I. Title.
TT835.B735   1997
746.46--dc21   98-4751
                                     CIP

Additional copies of this book may be ordered from: American Quilter's Society, PO Box 3290, Paducah, KY 42002-3290 @ $16 .95. Add $2.00 for postage & handling.

Copyright © 1997, Bonnie K. Browning

Printed in the U.S.A. by Image Graphics, Paducah, KY

Contents

Dedication

To all the quilters who have gone before me and shared their work and patterns; to all the quilters who now help carry on this tradition; and to all future quilters who have yet to learn the joy of making a quilt.

To my husband, Wayne, for being my best friend, and for understanding when I want to design or quilt at any hour of the day or night.

To my mother, Mary Kirkland, for teaching me that working with your hands can be a pleasure, how to sew on the old treadle sewing machine, and that I can do anything I really want to do.

Acknowledgments

It takes many people to produce a book. From the quilters who made the quilts, to the editing and production staff at the American Quilter's Society, it has been a pleasure working with each of you.

Special thanks go to:
the quilters who granted permission to use their beautiful quilts and border patterns: Linda L. Brown, Amy T. Chamberlin, Loretta Coblentz, Susan C. Derkacz, Leslie Fehling, Shoko Ferguson, Tish Fiet, Joan Haws, Valerie R. Kelley, Suzanne Marshall, Ruth H. McIver, Rita Ptacek, Linda M. Roy, Shirley J. Stutz, and Beatrice Walroth for the Kingston Heirloom Quilters. Without them, this book would not yet be a reality.

Meredith Schroeder, who continues to promote the art of quiltmaking in so many ways.

Lanette Ballard and Terry Williams, whose designing expertise made this book come alive, and Charles R. Lynch and Richard Walker, whose photographic expertise shows off the quilts so well.

Introduction

"It must be realized that the beauty of a pattern is not due so much to the nature of its elements as to the right use of them as units in a rhythmic scheme."
                    Archibald H. Christie, 1929

This book was written for two reasons; first, to look at the historical development of border designs, since the border is probably the oldest decoration, and second, to provide technical information and border patterns for quiltmakers who are making quilts today.

By studying ornaments, one learns that decorations include geometric designs (motifs formed by the rhythmical arrangements of dots and lines), natural forms (leaves, flowers and fruits, either as single motifs or in combination), and the animal and human forms. In addition to these elements, there are artificial objects (forms borrowed from art, technology, and science).

How did pattern work evolve from utilitarian beginnings into a decorative art form? In antiquity, while prehistoric man was shaping the first necessities of life, his work was already blossoming with decoration, primarily geometric in character. Designs were carved into handles of tools, on vessels and walls, and into many of the things they used in their daily lives. Figure 1 is an example of a prehistoric weapon found in Hungary. This weapon has been decorated with several geometric borders. One has to wonder

Figure 1
A drawing of a prehistoric weapon with several geometric designs. From **The Styles of Ornament**, Dover Publications, Inc.

whether these drawings were initially made as decoration or as part of some kind of utilitarian device. Whatever the reason might have been then, today we look at these designs as part of the development of decoration.

Interesting ready-made patterns sometimes appear as incidental results of technical processes, such as the patterns produced by English and Flemish arrangements of bricks in building walls (Fig. 2). It makes you wonder, which came first — the pattern or the putting together of the wall?

Figure 2
Two different designs formed by putting together brick walls.

For thousands of years, craftsmen and artists have used designs to decorate their surroundings. Were the markings found on fragments of prehistoric pottery put there as decoration or as a kind of pictorial communication to which modern man has no clue? It would be merely guess-work on our part to try to determine the hows and whys of these decorations on this type of utilitarian item.

Since prehistoric times, craftsmen have engaged in mimicry in both establishing patterns and varying them. With craftsmen of so many different disciplines, painting, carving, weaving, sculpture, etc., attempting to use the same ornaments, it is hard to say any one ornament is an independent idea. Artists and craftsmen

Figure 3
Doorway from the church of St. Stefano in Bologna. From *The Styles of Ornament*, Dover Publications, Inc.

tend to borrow elements from one another, and the various techniques utilized tend to cause variations in design. A specific design cannot always be translated exactly from one medium to another without causing some variation. Or, sometimes slight variations, perhaps thought to be improvements, can bring about astonishing changes.

Whether a specific design element had its beginnings in prehistoric times on a pottery fragment, or from antiquity, the Middle Ages, the Renaissance, or modern times, today we have unlimited designs to work with in our artistic endeavors. Throughout all of these periods, borders have played a major role in decoration. Figure 3 is an example of Italian Romanesque borders used in the construction of a doorway during the Middle Ages. (Quilters will recognize a variety of designs used today — stars, Celtic designs, spirals, Log Cabin-like designs, triangles, and squares, all used in borders.)

Borders belong in the category of framework. They are used to define, frame, enhance, or isolate a design, or to increase the size of the piece. It is interesting to follow the rise of borders on an architectural basis, its gradual transformation and adaptation to the products of the art industry. If you compare the architectural details from various lands in Figures 4 and 5, you can see dramatic differences in styles of decoration.

Ancient patterns include lines (bands), zigzag lines, triangles, tooth rows, stepping patterns, squares, stars, crosses, circles, S–borders, spirals, double spirals, rosettes, fleur de lis, wavy lines, festoons, and twists (Fig. 6, page 8). Most of these patterns have been adapted and are being used in quilts today.

With the advance in the intellectual development of mankind, artists acquired more technical skill, and ventured to make use of animals, plants, and finally the human figure itself, for ornamental purposes. Artisans began using borders in many of the things that touched their lives, from their clothing to buildings and their furnishings.

Figure 4
A window of open-worked plaster in the Mosque of El-Ashraf, ca. 15th century. This design uses both geometrical and natural decoration. From *The Styles of Ornament*, Dover Publications, Inc.

Borders are all around us. On furniture, the borders appear as edging or trims. Other places to look for borders are oriental rugs; murals, windows, and sculptures in churches; picture frames, jewelry, baskets, ironwork, wallpaper, and textiles of all kinds. These things have been around for a long time, and their border designs have been borrowed, copied, and passed on by artisans for future generations to enjoy. This must sound familiar to you, for quilters have for generations borrowed, copied, and passed on designs used in quiltmaking. What is most fascinating is that many of these designs, many of which can be traced to prehistoric times, are used in much the same style today as well as in generations of adaptations.

And so, with this brief backward glance at the elements of decoration, we acknowledge that the basic elements are ages old. There is nothing new about these basic designs. Rather, it is the way that we put them together that individualizes our designs.

Quilters today are paying more attention to the borders of their quilts, those finishing frames that complete their works. As you read through the General Information in Chapter 1, you will find many ideas for designing and stitching a quilt top accurately, so that the borders will fit.

Figure 5
This decorated window of the Royal Castle in Cracow, Poland, has narrow geometric borders that are almost overwhelmed by the shields and festoons, ca. 16th century. From *The Styles of Ornament*, Dover Publications, Inc.

Introduction

line

band

zig zag

triangles

squares

squares on point

tooth row

stepping patterns

stars

crosses

circles

s-borders

spirals

twists

double spirals

rosettes

scales

fleur de lis

wavy lines

festoons

Figure 6
Design elements used for hundreds of years.

The Border Primer, Chapter 2, provides instructions for choosing borders to complement the central design of your quilt. Borders can be made of simple bands, squares, rectangles, or diamonds used as single elements or in combination. Designs can be adapted to create appliquéd borders in whatever style you might choose. The design possibilities are endless.

In Chapter 3 you will find a variety of finishing touches to add to a quilt. Perhaps a Dogtooth border or a single line of embroidery will be the perfect finish to your next quilt.

The quilters featured in Chapter 4, Gallery & Patterns, were juried into the American Quilter's Society Quilt Show in Paducah, Kentucky. Their quilts were, in fact, the inspiration for this book. After the quilts were juried into the AQS Show, I reviewed the slides to prepare press releases. In reviewing the slides for the 1996 Show, my first reaction was what wonderful borders these quilters had stitched onto their quilts! The border patterns represent a cross section of the types of designs being used today and the variety of techniques being employed. There are patterns that can be used by quiltmakers of any skill level; some are geared for beginners, while others are challenging for more advanced quilters. Look for special tips these quilters have shared; they have already worked through many design decisions and their technical solutions for stitching the borders are included. You will also find some patterns for the designs I drew for the beginning of each of the chapters.

As a quiltmaker for 20 years and quilt judge for 15 years, I have seen thousands of quilts. One of the areas that seems to make a quilt either very good or perhaps just mediocre is the treatment of the borders and edges. It is my hope that you will use this book to help make your borders the correct size, make quilts that are flat and straight, and most of all, make beautiful borders on your own quilts!

Bonnie K. Browning

This German wine cooler by Ruhl features several borders. Notice how the acanthus leaves are used several times, on the top, the handles, and feet. Imagine how beautiful these borders would be on a quilt. From *The Styles of Ornament*, Dover Publications, Inc.

Chapter 1

General Information

Before we talk about adding borders to a quilt top, we will take a brief look at all of the phases of making a quilt and some of the questions we handle that affect the final outcome. Is the top straight? Do the edges lie flat? Are the sashing strips even and the rows in line? A good foundation will make your borders all the more effective.

As you read this section, remember there are no hard and fast rules that must be followed when making your quilts. There are any number of methods that can be used. Sometimes, though, there may be logical reasons for doing certain things. The following information will explain some of those reasons and tell why some methods are suggested.

Fern Leaf border, pattern on pages 120–123.

Designing the Quilt

Sketching vs. stitching

There are two schools of thought when designing a quilt — to sketch the design or to just start stitching without sketching. There are no right or wrong ways to design. It is more a matter of which method you are more comfortable using.

Sketching the design gives you an opportunity to work out scale and color and determine how to finish the edges of the quilt before cutting into your fabric. Many problems can be solved on paper, rather than wasting fabric or having to use the humility tool, the seam ripper. Some people can visualize how the pieces will look after they are stitched. Others need to see it on paper first. Computer programs, both special quilting programs and other drawing software, have made the design process much easier. Using the computer lets you design, change, color, or add fabric patterns with just a few clicks of the keys. The good old-fashioned pencil works, too!

On the other hand, sometimes it is that surprise element you discover after something has been stitched that makes a quilt special. There are times when you might want to sketch first. Other times you might want to get right into cutting the fabric and sewing it together.

Fabric selection

Quilters find the 100% cotton fabrics available today easy to handle and stitch into quilts. In choosing your fabric, designs, and patterns, you might want to consider how the fabric will be cut and used. If you choose a fabric that has a pattern that has obvious lines in the design, you will want to consider how the pieces are cut, if you want the design to be straight each time it is cut. Of course, there is nothing to say that you have to have the fabric design run true.

Sometimes having the design run in random patterns adds pizazz to a quilt. If you want to lead the eye in many different directions, you can let the line of the fabric do that.

If your design has triangles or is cut on the bias rather than on the straight of grain, you will need to take extra effort not to stretch the bias edges. Bias lines are active, both visually and technically, and they can cause many problems if you are not careful with them.

What can you do to prevent stretching problems? You can place the bias-edged fabric on the top as you feed the fabric through your sewing machine. The feed dogs will be pulling on the bottom piece of fabric, rather than the bias piece. Also take care when pressing, making sure you only lift the iron up and down without sliding it. The back and forth motion we use when ironing shirts can distort the fabric pieces after they are stitched. Try to press with the grain of the fabric to minimize the chance of causing distortion. This caution is not meant to discourage you from using special cuts that create bias edges. It is just to make you aware that these bias edges and triangles need special handling.

Whenever possible, you will want to place any bias edges so they can be sewn to a piece with a straight grain to add stability. Try to make the edges of your blocks on the straight of grain, and likewise, make the edges of the quilt top on the straight of grain. If you happen to have some bias edges on the quilt top, adding sashing or a border cut on the straight of grain will add stability, too.

Making the Quilt Top

Marking

Have you ever made a quilt and had it finish wider than you planned? This can be caused by the type of marking tool used. A sharp pointed white or silver pencil can be used effectively on dark fabrics, and a mechanical pencil makes a fine line on light fabrics. A dull pencil can make a wider stitching line and add up to $\frac{1}{20}$" to each piece (Fig. 1–1). For illustration purposes, if a quilt is made of 10 blocks, each containing six squares across, this $\frac{1}{20}$" variance can mean your quilt could be 3" larger than planned.

$$\frac{1}{20}" \times 60 \text{ squares} = 60/20 = 3"$$

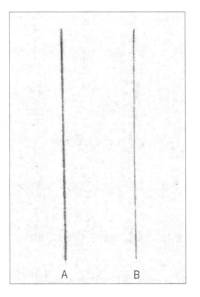

Figure 1–1
Comparison of stitching lines, marked with a dull pencil (A) and marked with a mechanical pencil (B).

For better accuracy, keep a sharp point on your pencil or use a fine-leaded mechanical pencil to trace the templates.

It is also important to stitch with a uniform seam allowance. If you are using rotary-cutting methods and a sewing machine, to determine $\frac{1}{4}$" seam allowance, place a ruler with the $\frac{1}{4}$"

mark on the ruler under the needle of your machine (Fig. 1–2). The edge of the ruler will be the line along which you should feed the fabric. You can place a piece of tape at the edge of the ruler to give you a handy guide to ensure an accurate seam allowance. Or, you can purchase a special foot for stitching $\frac{1}{4}$" seam allowances, available in quilt shops.

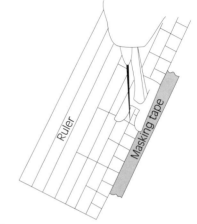

Figure 1–2
Determine an accurate $\frac{1}{4}$" seam allowance on your machine.

Piecing

If a quilt top is pieced and stitched by hand or marked for machine piecing, the choice of marking tool may affect the accuracy of the blocks. As you stitch the pieces of the block together, check to see if your stitching is on the seam line on both pieces. If it is not, take care to pin the pieces together. Use a positioning pin to mark the first corner, then place a pin in the next corner (Fig. 1–3). Pull both pins until the heads rest against the top fabric. Now, both layers are securely held in place. Using a third pin,

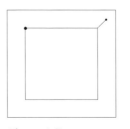

Figure 1–3
Place a positioning pin at each corner.

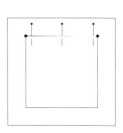

Figure 1–4
Pin every 1" or 2" along the seam line.

take a small bite of fabric to hold the layers together for stitching. Place a pin every one or two inches across the seam line to be stitched (Fig. 1–4). This method can be used for either hand stitching or for precision machine stitching, in which the line of stitches starts where the seam lines cross and the seam allowances are not stitched. If the seam allowances are not stitched, it gives some freedom in how the allowances can be pressed. For instance, if you press a block and notice that the tip of a point has been lost in the seam, you can try pressing the allowances to the other side, or even open, to expose the tip.

Appliqué

For appliquéd quilts, cutting the background block at least an inch larger than the desired finished size will make it possible to square up each block after the appliqué has been completed. Often, the appliqué stitching will take up some of the fabric. Having an extra allowance to trim off after it is appliquéd is just a bit of insurance to make sure the block is not too small.

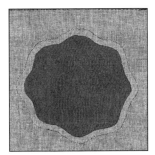

Figure 1–5
Trim the background behind the appliqué, leaving a ¼" seam allowance.

If the background puckers slightly around the applique, it is probably because you have pulled the thread a bit more than necessary. In order to release this tension, remove the background behind the applique by cutting around the shape, leaving a ¼" allowance (Fig. 1–5).

Setting the blocks together

Before setting the blocks together, be sure to measure each one for uniformity. If one or two blocks are inaccurate, now is the time to fix them. Check your seam allowances. Are they

the same? If not, rip out the seam and restitch it. Remember, if the blocks are not the same size now, they will have to be stretched or scrunched to fit them together. This can cause unevenness in your quilt and it may not lie flat. A little time making these corrections now will make completing the quilt easier.

Sashing

Do you just cut a strip of fabric and sit down to sew your blocks to it, one after the other, in assembly-line fashion? This is one typical reason a quilt does not lie completely flat. When you place the strip on the bottom, it is pulled through by the feed dogs, while the block lies on top and goes along for the ride. This can cause more fabric to be fed through on the bottom layer, making the sashing slightly larger than the block. A better way is to measure the size of the block and cut strips the length to fit from corner to corner on the block. Accurate measuring of all sashing strips is important in keeping your quilt top straight and flat.

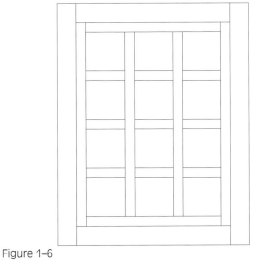

Figure 1–6
Short sashing strips run horizontally with long sashing strips connecting the rows vertically. Your eye is led down the quilt.

Sashing can be added with the short strips running either horizontally or vertically. If you are making a bed quilt, you might want the short strips running horizontally, so the long vertical sashing will run the length of the bed, leading the eye down the bed's length without any breaks (Fig. 1–6, page 13). Or, if you want to lead the eye across a wallhanging, you might want the longer strips going in a horizontal direction (Fig. 1–7). This is a design decision you can make. There are no hard and fast rules, although you may read that it must be done one way or the other. Every quilt is different and you can lead the viewer's eye as you choose by the placement of your sashing strips.

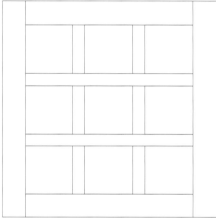

Figure 1–7
Short sashing strips run vertically, with long sashing strips connecting rows horizontally. Your eye is led across the quilt.

Short sashing strips should be cut the width of the blocks. Stitch the blocks into rows, matching the corners of the blocks and the sashing strips. Measure the complete row of blocks. The long sashing should be cut to that measurement. To ensure the blocks will line up from one row to the next, mark the wrong side of the long strip, with chalk or a pencil, with the same measurements as the sewn strip of blocks (Fig. 1–8). Note that the top and bottom blocks will be ¼" longer than the finished block size because you still have seam allowances on those edges. These marks provide a line to pin the seams of the blocks to ensure they line up as the rows are stitched together.

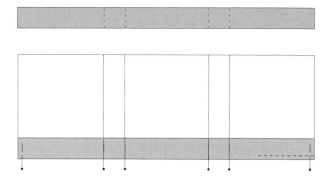

Figure 1–8
Mark the long sashing strips to align the blocks before the rows are stitched together.

Borders

Detailed information for adding borders is included in Chapter 2, Border Primer.

Quilting the Quilt

Quilting designs

Choose quilting designs that will complement the quilt top. It is important to plan the design so there will be approximately the same amount of quilting over the whole quilt. This does not mean the same design must be used over the entire quilt. For example, if you stipple quilt in the center of the quilt, be sure to do some in the corners and/or borders of the quilt too. Sometimes we work so hard quilting the center of the quilt that by the time we get to the borders, we want to get finished and skimp on the quilting there. The result may be that the quilt does not lie flat, and the edges may be wobbly.

If you have selected a busy print, save your beautiful quilting designs for open areas where they will be visible (Fig. 1–9). Straight-line quilting is effective on busy prints and is easier to stitch.

Feathered wreaths and cables can make a quilt special. Remember to vary the scale of the background quilting so it is either smaller or

Figure 1-9
Quilting design does not show well on busy fabrics.

spaced closer or wider than the width of the feather. This spacing will help show off the feathers, and let the background quilting be seen as well. When the spacing is nearly the same scale, neither the feathers nor the background quilting is shown to its best advantage.

Basting

One often overlooked preparation for quilting is basting the layers together. The purpose of basting is to hold the layers together as you stitch. If a quilt has too little basting, you will have to use your quilting needle to help pull the layers together. If you think this is a place you can save some time, don't skip this step. It is well worth the effort to have the quilt well-basted so the layers are securely held together as you quilt to eliminate puckers.

Common methods for basting include taping the backing to tables (enough tables to accommodate the entire top) or to a floor. Then the batting and quilt top can be pinned to the backing.

Here is how to baste on a carpet:
1. Cut the backing fabric 6"–8" larger than your quilt top (that is 3"–4" on all sides).

larger than the scale of the feathers (Figs. 1–10 and 1–11). You can see how varying the scale makes the feathers more prominent. One rule of thumb is to make sure the background quilting is

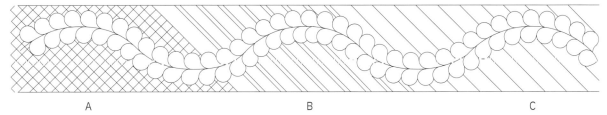

    A   B   C

Figure 1–10
(A) Background quilting smaller in scale than the quilted motif, (B) varied spacing still shows off feathers, and (C) spacing of background quilting is too close to the size of the feathers.

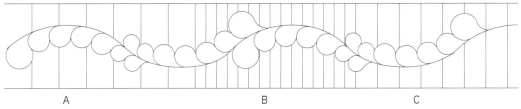

    A   B   C

Figure 1–11
(A) Background quilting larger in scale than the quilted motif, (B) background is smaller in scale, and (C) shows the feathers and background too close in size.

2. Spread the backing fabric on your carpet, wrong side up, and smooth it out. Begin to pin it in place by placing straight pins at an angle through the backing into the carpet. Start pinning on one side, then move to the opposite side until you have the entire backing pinned to the carpet.

3. Spread the batting over the backing and smooth out any lumps or tucks (Fig. 1–12A). Place a few pins at the edges just to keep the batting in place while you adjust the quilt top. It helps to take the batting out of its package a day ahead. Spread it on a bed or sofa. Moisture from the air will help relax the batting fibers, eliminate wrinkles, and make it easier to spread. If you forget to take it out of the package before you are ready to use it, you can place it in a dryer on "air" for just a couple of minutes. (Be sure that the dryer is not hot or you could melt polyester batting.)

4. Center the quilt top, right side up, over the batting. Pin in place through the carpet like you did for the backing. Use a ruler and/or square to make sure the lines of your design are kept straight. Check the corners to make sure they are square.

5. Use a long needle (basting, sharp, or darning) and basting or other white thread.

Sometimes we like to use odd bits of thread for basting. Remember, if that thread has color in it, it also has dye to make it that color. Under the right conditions, dye can rub off on your quilt from the colored thread. White or off-white thread is recommended to remove any risk of dye transferring to the quilt.

6. Start in the center of the quilt and baste one quarter of the quilt in both directions, stitching from the center to the edge of the quilt (Fig. 1–12B). When starting a line of stitching, take a backstitch instead of knotting the thread. Backstitch to end a line of stitching, too. These backstitches make it easy to remove the basting. Using a teaspoon to lift the needle as you baste will save you a good deal of time (Fig. 1–12C). You can develop a good rhythm by twisting your hand to lift the needle, making the basting go faster.

7. After all four quarters are basted, run a line of basting around the edges (Fig 1–12D). If you are going to quilt in a hoop, fold the backing to the front, encasing the edges of the quilt, and baste in place. This will protect the edges while you handle the quilt during the quilting process.

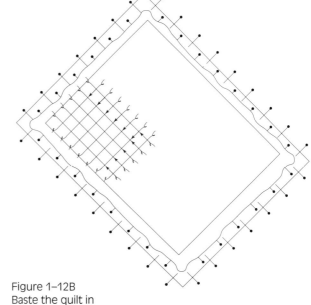

Figure 1–12B
Baste the quilt in quarter sections.

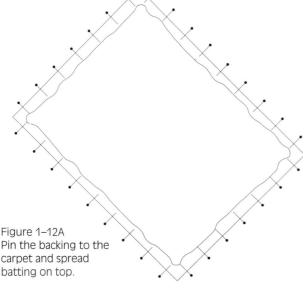

Figure 1–12A
Pin the backing to the carpet and spread batting on top.

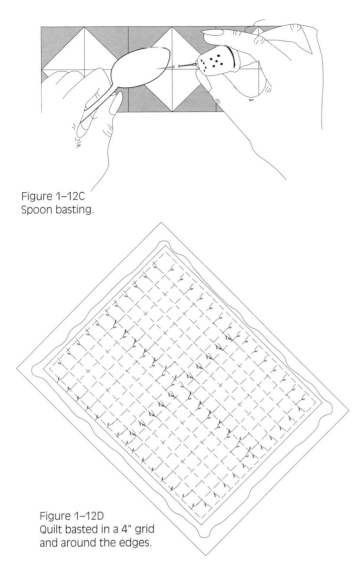

Figure 1–12C
Spoon basting.

Figure 1–12D
Quilt basted in a 4" grid
and around the edges.

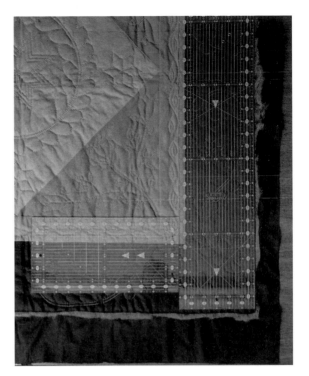

Figure 1–13
Make sure the corners are square by aligning one ruler with a seam on the quilt and a second ruler along the edge to be trimmed. Amish quilt by Sara Newberg King.

The basting stitches can be removed as you complete a section. It is fun to see the dimension the quilting adds as you progress.

Working on the Edge

Trimming

After the quilting has been finished, it is time to finish the edge of the quilt. Measure the quilt before you do any final trimming of the edges.

Using a square and ruler (or two rulers) and chalk, pencil, or pins to mark a line for trimming the edges of the quilt. Make sure the corners are square and the edges straight (Fig. 1–13).

Measure again to make sure the measurements are the same across the top, the center, and the bottom of the quilt (Fig. 1–14, page 18). Measure down the quilt to check the measurements in the same three areas. A quick way to check these measurements is to fold both sides of the quilt toward the center, checking all three measurements at once. Turn the quilt and check the measurements in the opposite direction.

Sometimes, a design element, such as a pieced design that goes to the edge of the quilt, will prevent cutting off enough to make the edge straight. Trimming it down would cut off part of the seam allowance, and then part of the design would be stitched into the seam. If this is the case and one side is a little longer than the other, try running a basting thread along the edge to ease the longer side to the same measurement as the other.

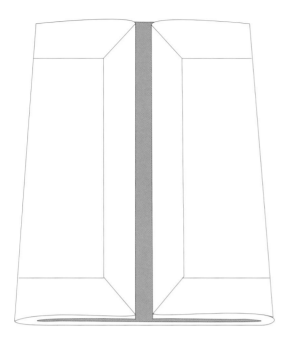

Figure 1–14
Checking the measurements at top, center, and bottom across the quilt.

Binding

Binding can be made from a single or double layer of fabric. Because the binding is usually the first part of a quilt to show wear, you may want to use a double layer of binding for bed quilts. For wallhangings or clothing, a single layer may be sufficient.

Another question that is often asked — should the binding be on the straight of grain or the bias? The answer is, it can be either. Let's look at the fabric for each type of cut.

The straight-cut fabric will have long threads running up and down, with only a few threads on the edge of the quilt. If one of those edge threads is broken, that portion of the edge will be weakened (Fig. 1–15).

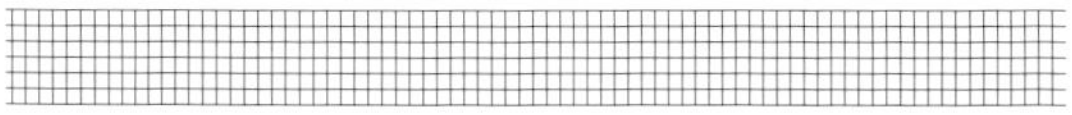

Figure 1–15
Long threads running lengthwise on the edge of the binding.

If a bias strip is used for the binding, and one thread is broken, because there are so many more threads running along the edge of the quilt, little damage will have been done to the integrity of the bias edge (Fig. 1–16). Therefore, the use of bias-cut binding helps to make the binding wear better.

Figure 1–16
Threads running on the bias edge of the binding.

Make your binding from bias strips 2¼" wide. Sew enough strips together, end to end, to encircle the quilt plus at least 15". Cut a 45° angle on one end (Fig. 1–17). Fold the strip in half lengthwise, wrong sides together. Lay the raw edge of the binding along the raw edge of the quilt top, starting about 7" to 10" from a lower corner. (For a smoother finish, use your sewing machine to sew the binding.) Leave the beginning 4" unsewn to aid in joining the ends after the binding has been stitched around the entire quilt.

Figure 1–17
Cut a 45° angle at the beginning end of the binding strip.

At the corner, place a pin ¼" from the edge of the quilt top. Begin stitching, using a scant ¼" seam allowance (Fig. 1–18). Stitch until you reach the pin; then take a couple of backstitches. Raise the presser foot and cut the threads. Fold the binding up to form a 45° angle in the corner (Fig. 1–19). Next fold the binding down along the second edge, making sure the fold is even with the edge of the quilt at the corner (Fig. 1–20). Place a pin ¼" from the second corner.

18

Begin stitching at the corner and continue until you come to the pin again. Backstitch and cut the threads. Stitch the binding on the third side in the same manner. On the fourth side, start stitching from the corner and stop stitching about 4" to 6" from where you started. To join the ends, smooth the tail end along the raw

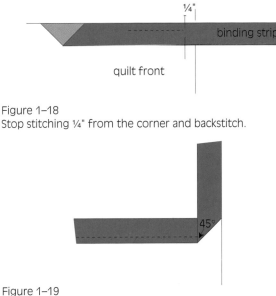

Figure 1–18
Stop stitching ¼" from the corner and backstitch.

Figure 1–19
Remove from machine and fold the binding to form 45° angle in corner.

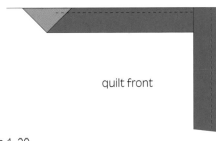

Figure 1–20
Begin stitching at the edge.

edge of the quilt (Fig. 1–21). Now lay the beginning end with the 45° cut (called a miter) on top of the tail end. Make a pencil mark on the tail where the edge of the miter starts. If you were to draw a matching miter on the tail at this mark, the two pieces would only meet. You need seam allowances for both ends. From the first mark, place a second mark on the tail end ½" (that is two ¼" allowances) away from the first mark (Fig. 1–22). Open the beginning miter out flat so you

can see which direction the miter goes. Using that as a guide, place your ruler on the tail end to mark a miter in the same direction. Cut off excess binding, on the drawn line.

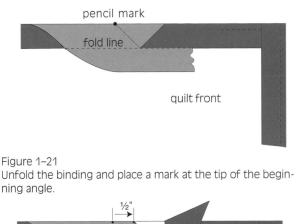

Figure 1–21
Unfold the binding and place a mark at the tip of the beginning angle.

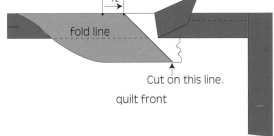

Figure 1–22
Add ½" allowances and draw a 45° angle on the tail end.

Now, with the binding opened flat, stitch the two mitered ends, right sides together, and finger press the seam allowance open (Fig. 1–23). Fold the binding in half again and stitch the remaining section to the quilt. This method gives you a very neat finish to your binding.

Fig. 1–23
Join right sides together and stitch using ¼" seam allowance.

Fold the binding over to the back side of the quilt and blindstitch it in place by hand (Fig. 1–24). Make sure the stitching line is covered. Also remember to stitch the mitered corners closed on both the front and back of the quilt.

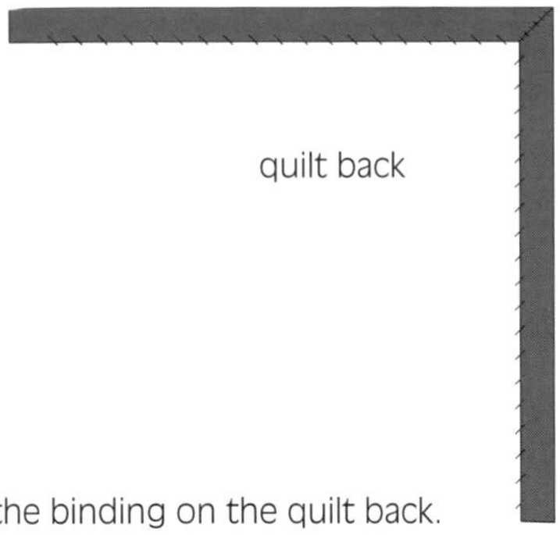

Figure 1–24
Blindstitch the binding on the quilt back.

quilt back

An easy way to remember to do this is to stitch until you get to the corner, fold the mitered corner in place and take a tacking stitch at the base of the miter. Slide your needle through to the front and stitch along the miter to the corner; at the top, slide your needle to the back and stitch down the back of the miter. Continue blindstitching the binding.

Do you always need to make mitered corners on the binding? It is important to be consistent in the elements of a quilt. If the borders are mitered, a mitered binding will continue that design element better than a binding that has been squared at the corners. If a block has been set into the corner of the border, using a squared corner in the binding would keep the corners consistent.

To stitch the squared corner binding, attach strips of binding to the front top and bottom edges. Trim the ends to form square corners. Fold the binding to the back and blindstitch it in place (Fig. 1–25).

Figure 1–25
Binding strip added to the top of the quilt.

Stitch binding to the sides of the quilt, leaving ½" beyond the corners. Fold in the ½", making sure the corner is still square. Wrap the binding to the back and blindstitch in place (Fig. 1–26). Be sure to stitch closed the folded ends of the binding to help make the binding more secure.

Fig. 1–26
Corners of the binding will form 90° angles.

Quilts with irregular edges, like Grandmother's Flower Garden or Double Wedding Ring, may be finished in a variety of ways. They can be bound with binding. (Remember that any curves will require a bias binding to fold around the curve properly.) Another option is to fold the edges of both the front and back in and blindstitch the edge. A separate facing can be made from a strip of fabric and laid right sides together onto the quilt top. Stitch along the irregular edges, clip along curves and indentations, turn, and whip in place on the back side of the quilt.

Sometimes the edges of a quilt will wobble (not lay completely flat). After the binding has been completely stitched to the front and back of the quilt, try quilting in the ditch along the binding. This extra row of stitching through all the layers may help stabilize the edges.

Once you have completed the binding, you are ready to put a label with your name, city, state, date, and any other information you wish, on the back of your quilt.

Chapter 2

Border Primer

Does every quilt need a border? The answer to that question is "no." To border or not to border your quilt is one of the design decisions you must make. A border can be added for several reasons —

> to enhance the center of the quilt,
> to define a section or the whole quilt,
> to provide a frame,
> to bring out the colors in the design,
> to stop the design in the center, or
> to enlarge the size of the quilt.

The color of the border plays an important role. A dark border has the effect of lightening and enlarging the quilt center, while a light frame serves to darken and shrink the image.

Rigid detail is denoted by formal geometric lines, while natural shapes (vines, flowers, etc.) lend free and spontaneous lines. Between these two extremes there are infinite gradations from relaxed to formal designs. The design is our own decision. We can take what we have learned from history and our own experience and just do it! The results are our own personal statements stitched into our quilts.

Making the Borders Fit

Before beginning any borders, we have to know how to make a border that will accurately fit the quilt top. If you are adding a pieced border, begin by measuring the top and bottom edges and across the center of the quilt to determine the length of the top and bottom borders. If these three measurements are not the same, check the seam allowances used in assembling the quilt top. If the difference is ½" or less, average the three measurements together and make the border that length (Fig. 2–1). You can easily fudge ½" to fit the pieced borders, either by stretching or gathering the fabric slightly. You will also need to measure the sides and down the center of the quilt to determine the length of the side borders.

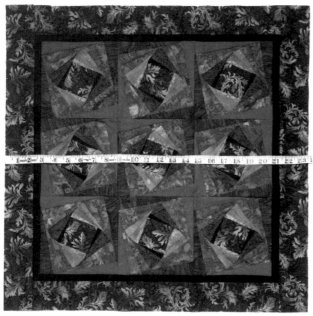

Fig. 2–1
Measure the quilt center to determine length of border.

If the difference is more than ½", it is best to stop here and find out why. Measure the blocks — are they the same size? Are the sashing strips the same width? Fix any blocks that need to be restitched before you go on with the borders.

If the space must be divided to accommodate the design, you have to determine what the increments will be. In the *Encyclopedia of Designs for Quilting*, Phyllis Miller suggests, for a square quilt, cutting a piece of paper the length of the border by the exact finished width of the quilt. Include the corner square of the border when cutting the paper. The border may not have an actual square sewn in and, if not, simply allow for a square. With a pencil and ruler, draw a line where this square would be (Fig. 2–2). For a rectangular quilt, cut one piece of paper for the border length and another piece of paper for the border width.

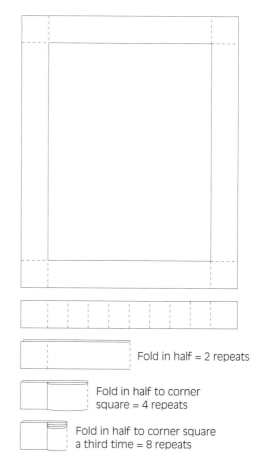

Fold in half = 2 repeats

Fold in half to corner square = 4 repeats

Fold in half to corner square a third time = 8 repeats

Fig. 2–2
Fold the paper to determine sections in a border.

First, fold the paper in half up to the line where a corner square would be. Fold this section in half again. Keep folding the paper in half until you reach a size that accommodates your design. You will find there is less distortion in folding if you fold accordion style, rather than continuing to fold the paper over on itself.

This method is best suited to appliquéd borders because the background sections are usually larger, but it could also be used to determine the block size required for a pieced border. For pieced borders it is usually easier to figure the block size mathematically; that is, a quilt border 64" wide could have eight 8" blocks, sixteen 4" blocks, or thirty-two 2" blocks. If you cannot arrive at a block dimension that is easy to handle, you might want to consider adding a narrow single band border to the quilt top to make the dimensions easier to subdivide.

Sometimes the spacing will not come out even. There might be $\frac{1}{16}$" or $\frac{1}{8}$" left over. Some designs lend themselves to reversing the design at the center of the border. If you have a fraction left over, it may be less visible if it is added to the squares in the center where the design reverses, or you can add it at the corners.

If the quilt is a rectangle, you will need to make a pattern for the top and bottom, and a second pattern for the sides. The divisions may not be exactly the same but visually these small variations should not be distracting. One way to camouflage any variations is to include a design element in the center of each side; the design can be larger or smaller as needed to fit the area. If you look at A Quilt for Kristen on page 91, you will see the type of design element that can be used in the center of each side. More flowers have been used on the sides than on the top and bottom to fit the space and still be in scale with the border size.

Border Designs

A quilt does not have to have a border, but if you decide it needs one, you will want to choose a design that enhances the center of the quilt. Sometimes, a simple border is enough. Other times, a more complicated border may be the pièce de résistance.

No border

Log Cabin quilts often do not have borders (Fig. 2–3). Quilts that are set on point with alternating plain blocks (Fig. 2–4, page 24) and one-patch quilts are also good examples of typically borderless quilts. Blocks that create an irregular edge, such as Double Wedding Ring, Baby Blocks, or Grandmother's Flower Garden, are also often made without borders (Fig. 2–5, page 24).

Figure 2–3
Log Cabin quilt with no border.

Figure 2–4
Blocks set on point create the look of a border without adding one.

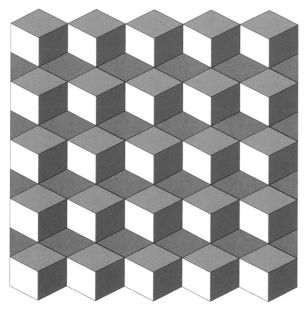

Figure 2–5
Irregular edges create interest without adding an additional border.

Changing color value

The color scheme of the blocks can be changed to simulate a border (Fig. 2–6). You can simply change the value of parts of the blocks on the edges to create a border-like design. Remember to adapt the corner blocks.

Figure 2–6
Changing the color scheme at the edge of the quilt simulates a border without adding one.

Single bands

A single-band border can help frame or contain the motion of the central part (body) of the quilt, and it can finish a busy quilt without overpowering the central design. This is the simplest border that can be added. All you need to decide is the border width. To help keep the width in scale, try using a dimension from the blocks used in the quilt; that is, use 2", 3", 4", or 6" border if 12" blocks were used (Fig. 2–7).

For butted corners, cut the top and bottom borders as long as the quilt body is wide. The side borders are cut the length of the quilt plus twice the width of the border, plus ½" for seam allowances.

24

Figure 2–7
A single band contains the motion in the quilt.

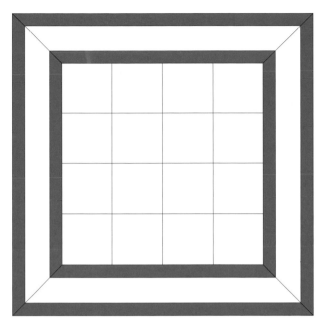

Figure 2–8
Using dimensions of the block keeps the multiple band borders in scale.

> Border cutting formula:
> Top & bottom borders = width of the quilt
> Side borders = length of quilt + 2x width of border + ½" for seam allowances

Multiple bands

Multiple bands can add another design element and provide a more substantial frame to a quilt. To determine the size of the bands, use a dimension from the blocks; that is, if 15" blocks are used in the quilt, 3" (⅕ of block), 5" (⅓), 7½" (½), or 10" (⅔) borders would appear in scale with the rest of the quilt top. If three bands are used together, they could be 3", 7½", and 3" (Fig. 2–8); or 3", 5", and 10" could be used if a wider border is desired. Multiple bands can be cut individually and added to the quilt one at a time, or they can be cut, stitched together, and added as a unit (Fig. 2–9). If you stitch them together, calculate the length of each border carefully, using the border cutting formula.

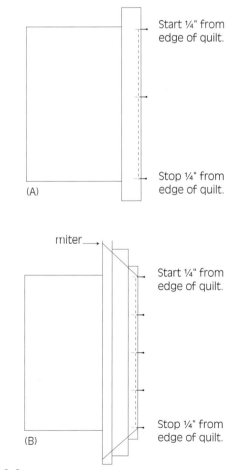
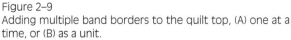

(A) Start ¼" from edge of quilt. Stop ¼" from edge of quilt.

miter (B) Start ¼" from edge of quilt. Stop ¼" from edge of quilt.

Figure 2–9
Adding multiple band borders to the quilt top, (A) one at a time, or (B) as a unit.

Geometric designs

When geometric ornaments are used in the border, try selecting elements that are used in the blocks to help continue the design from the center to the edges. For pieced blocks with triangles, use some of the same triangles in the border (Fig. 2–10). The triangles could be resized, made smaller or larger, but the design element would be the same.

Figure 2–10
Repeating triangles in the border ties the border to the central design of the quilt.

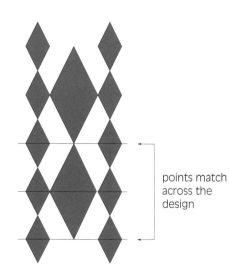

Figure 2–11
The repeat of the larger border matches the divisions of the smaller border.

points match
across the
design

If multiple geometric borders are used, it is good to have some relation between the repeats of the designs. Where the repeat is apparent, they should divide one into the other (Fig. 2–11).

Squares

Simple alternating squares in two or more colors can make an effective border (Fig. 2–12). Multiple rows of squares make a checkerboard border. A border using squares looks attractive with a single band border on either side. If you use one color on one side and a second color on the other side of the squares, you create a tooth-like border.

(A) Single row of squares.

(B) Multiple rows of squares make a checkerboard border.

(C) Using single bands on both sides forms tooth row border

Figure 2–12
Examples of borders using squares. (A) Single row of squares, alternating colors; (B) multiple rows of squares make a checkerboard border; (C) using single bands on both sides of a single row of squares forms a tooth row border.

Spaced squares

Squares alternating with rectangles can add more variety than using only squares (Fig. 2–13). Sometimes breaking up the squares with a rectangular shape interrupts the regularity of the design and adds interest.

(A)

(B)

(C)

Figure 2–13
Add variety by alternating squares with rectangles. (A) Two colors of squares with a rectangle; (B) squares and rectangles in a single row; and (C) multiple rows create a brick-like geometric border.

Divided squares

Drawing a parallelogram inside a square can be used to create ribbon-like borders (Fig. 2–14).

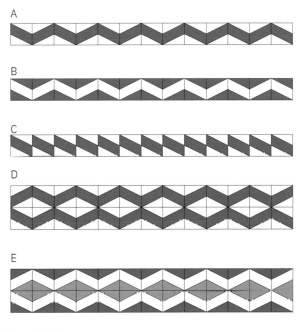

A

B

C

D

E

Figure 2–14
Ribbon-like designs from divided squares. (A) Dark ribbon with light background; (B) light ribbon with dark background; (C) repeating the block, without turning the blocks; (D) mirror image rows with light background; and (E) mirror image rows using three colors.

Triangles

The bias lines of triangles can add motion to a border. Sometimes a sawtooth or dogtooth border can be just the addition a quilt needs (Fig. 2–15). Figures 2–15A – H show several variations that can be achieved with a single triangular block. Notice how the the design changes even though the same simple block is used. Putting two or more simple blocks together can make an intricate-looking border.

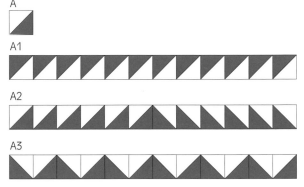

A

A1

A2

A3

Figure 2–15 (A)
(A) Simple half-square triangle block; (A1) sawtooth border repeats block; (A2) sawtooth, reversed at center of border; and (A3) Flying Geese are formed by matching light corners of the blocks.

B

B1

B2

B3

B4

B5

B6

Figure 2–15 (B)
(B) Isosceles triangle; (B1) repeat block; (B2) reverse every other block; (B3) make the light or the dark triangles more prominent, depending on which side is attached to the edge of the quilt top; (B4) turn the blocks to create an asymmetrical border; (B5) reverse every other block; and (B6) reverse every two blocks.

C

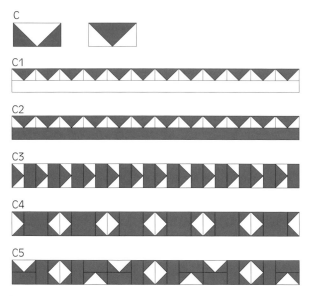

C1

C2

C3

C4

C5

Figure 2–15 (C)

(C) Flying Geese block; (C1) repeat block, add a single light border; (C2) repeat block, add a single dark border; (C3) alternate with a dark rectangle; (C4) form a square with two blocks back-to-back, alternate with a solid dark square; and (C5) add a dark rectangle to make a square, turn blocks to create an asymmetrical border.

D

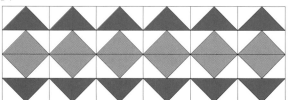

D1

D2

Figure 2–15 (D)

(D) Double Flying Geese block; (D1) mirror image two rows of blocks; and (D2) turn block sideways, repeat a second row pointing in opposite direction.

E

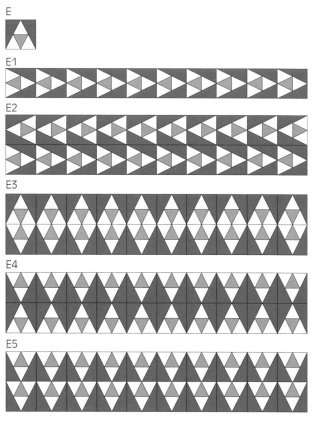

E1

E2

E3

E4

E5

Figure 2–15 (E)

(E) Pieced triangle block; (E1) repeat block, all in the same direction; (E2) two rows of blocks, with each row of triangles pointing in opposite directions; (E3) two rows, mirror imaged, with dark triangles on the outside edges; (E4) similar to (E3), but with light triangles on the outside edges; and (E5) two rows, with triangles placed in the same direction.

F

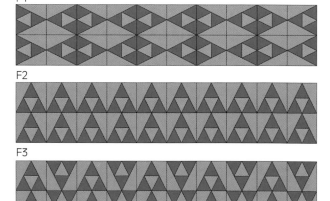

F1

F2

F3

Figure 2–15 (F)

(F) Low contrast colors in pieced triangle block; (F1) two rows, reversing every other block; (F2) two rows, repeat blocks; and (F3) two rows, reversing every other block.

G

G1

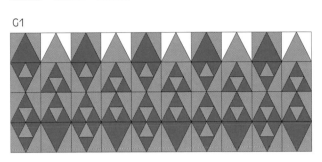

Figure 2–15 (G)
(G) Border units, and (G1) combine the units to create an intricate-looking, yet easy-to-make border.

H

H1

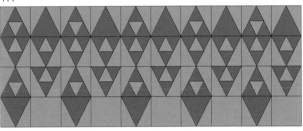

H2

Figure 2–15 (H)
(H) Wider borders can be created by combining several units in multiple rows; (H1) four rows of units in asymmetrical border; (H2) six rows of units in symmetrical border.

Stretching design into border

Continuing a portion of the quilt center can complete a design element and create an interesting border as well. Figure 2–16 shows how completing a design from the center of the quilt adds interest to an otherwise plain border. Plain corner areas can be used for a more elaborate quilting design.

Figure 2–16
Sometimes, completing a design in the border area is a good way to finish the quilt.

Appliquéd borders

Creating a design that is in proportion to the quilt center, making it fit the edges, and turning the corners are the challenges of making appliquéd borders.

Appliquéd borders can be designed to travel in one direction around the quilt, to reverse at the midpoint of each border (Fig. 2–17), or to flow out from the corners (Fig. 2–18, page 30). The design can also begin at the miter or square of the corner and flow to the next corner (Fig. 2–19, page 30), requiring a plain corner or design to fill it. Flexibility is definitely a key word when describing appliquéd borders. Flowers, vines, and other designs from nature let you use your own creativity in stitching appliquéd borders.

Figure 2–17
The design reverses at the center of the border.

Figure 2–18
The design flows from the corner into adjoining borders.

Figure 2–19
The design covers the edge without going into the corners.

Figures 2–20, 2–21, and 2–22 show some ideas for placement of vines, from zigzags to shallow, undulating lines. The design looks best if it covers the width of the border, leaving a narrow margin (½" to 1") at each edge. The width of the margin will depend on the width of the border.

Figure 2–20
Zigzag, using straight lines.

Figure 2–21
Undulating vine, with flowing arcs.

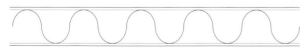

Figure 2–22
Undulating vine, with arcs spaced closer together.

Undulating vines have long been used as border designs. They can be as simple or complex as you like. Figure 2–23 shows four steps to developing a design that could be used as a simple vine and berries, one with simple flowers, flowers and leaves, or a complex floral design.

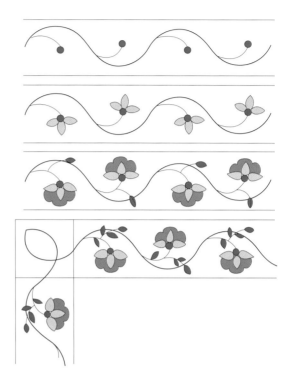

Figure 2–23
The development stages of an undulating vine design.

Festoons (swags) of fruit tied with leaves and flowers were popular during the Roman, Renaissance, and later periods. Originally, real fruit was hung as decoration on the friezes of temples. Later, fruit was included as part of the architecture of buildings. Swags can be designed as single pieces, divided either horizontally or vertically, scalloped, or overlapped (Fig. 2–24).

Sometimes, a swag design might not meet exactly at the edge of the corner square. If this happens, make the design fit the space and connect the swags on the two sides or add a design element in the center of each border to help fill the space. Adding a flower, bow, or other motif where the swags meet will cover any inaccuracies.

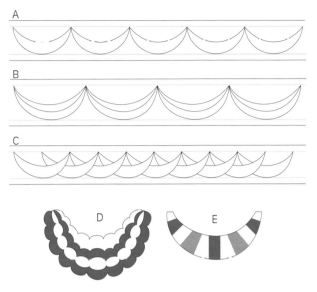

Figure 2–24
(A) Single swag; (B) double swag; (C) overlapped swag; (D) scalloped swag — notice how it reverses to scallop the top edge too; and (E) pieced swag.

If an appliquéd border is used with a pieced quilt center, using some of the fabrics from the blocks in the appliqué will help to tie the borders to the center part of the quilt.

Using striped fabrics for borders can add interest without having to piece or appliqué the border. Usually the design is matched at mitered corners to continue the flow of the border design (Fig. 2–25). Sometimes, a narrow band will need to be added to the quilt top so that the print can be matched.

Figure 2–25
Miter the corners and match the design of a border print.

The border print can also be cut off and butted against another border (Fig. 2–26).

Figure 2–26
Using a border print in straight borders.

Corner Treatments

Once you have decided on a border design, the next question is how to turn the corners. Pieced designs are perhaps easier than appliquéd borders because you can place a block in the corner to continue the design. That block can be plain, a pieced design from the interior of the quilt, or another design that helps to carry the eye around the corner. Of course, some quilters prefer different designs on every border, and in that case, there may be no common corner block. Figures 2–27 and 2–28, page 32, show examples of corner blocks.

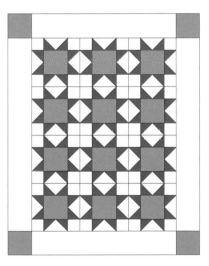

Figure 2–27
A plain block used in the corner.

Figure 2–28
A design using elements from the quilt top for the corner block. Notice how this design helps to carry your eye around the corner and also ties the quilt center and border together.

The corner treatment in an appliquéd border can be handled in several ways. The corner design can be a continuation of the design of the border. It can use a circular, elliptical, triangular, or heart shape to connect the designs (Figs. 2–29, 2–30, 2–31, 2–32). Or, the corners can be left blank (no design) to make the other border design more important. Figure 2–33 shows a variety of corners for pieced borders.

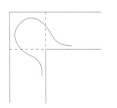

Figure 2–29
A circular design connects the borders.

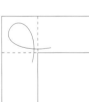

Figure 2–30
An elliptical shape can form a corner design.

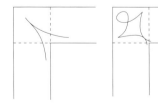

Figure 2–31
Triangular shapes connect the borders.

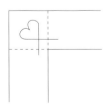

Figure 2–32
Heart shape in corner.

Figure 2–33
Several examples of borders with corners designed to continue the flow and lead the eye around the quilt.

Borders & Finishing Touches

Stitching the Corners

How to stitch the corners of the quilt is another design decision. Corners can be squared, mitered, shaped, or even split.

Squared corners

When a plain square or a pieced square is added to the corners, this is called a squared corner. The top, bottom, and side borders are cut to fit those edges. The additional squares are added to either the top and bottom or the side borders before those two borders are added to the quilt (Fig. 2–34).

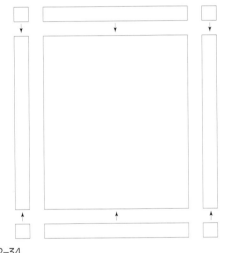

Figure 2–34
Assembling borders with corner squares.

Mitered corners

Mitered corners are often used when bands, multiple bands, or appliquéd borders are added. When the design is being carried around the corner, as in appliqué, one less seam is involved if you use a miter in the corner. It is important that the borders be cut accurately to fit the edges of the quilt top so the miters will lay flat. Excess fabric at the corners can make what are called dog-eared corners — ones that stick up and out from the straight edges of the quilt.

Figure 2–35 shows the steps for marking and stitching a mitered corner.

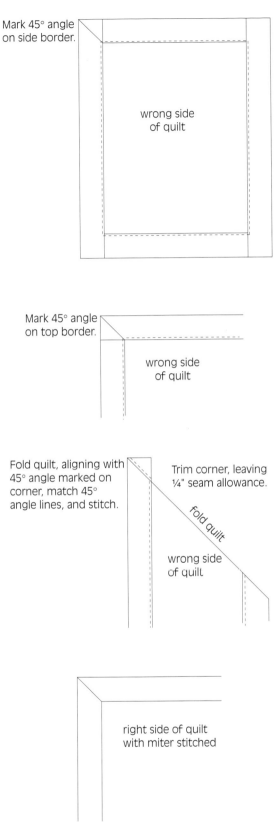

Mark 45° angle on side border.

wrong side of quilt

Mark 45° angle on top border.

wrong side of quilt

Fold quilt, aligning with 45° angle marked on corner, match 45° angle lines, and stitch.

Trim corner, leaving ¼" seam allowance.

fold quilt

wrong side of quilt

right side of quilt with miter stitched

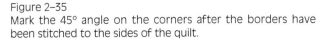

Figure 2–35
Mark the 45° angle on the corners after the borders have been stitched to the sides of the quilt.

Shaped corners

Some designs call for the corners to be round-ed. An easy way to make that curve is to take a large dinner plate, lay it in the corner, and draw around it (Fig. 2–36). Remember to use a bias binding if you choose a curved edge for your quilt.

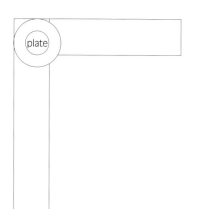

Figure 2–36
Use a dinner plate to make a rounded corner.

Split corners

Beds with corner posts require the bottom of the quilt be split to properly fit the end of the bed. To do this, determine the drop on the side of the bed and cut out a square from both bot-tom corners to that measurement (Fig. 2–37). Then the bottom of the quilt will fit between the bed posts and the sides will drop neatly over the edges.

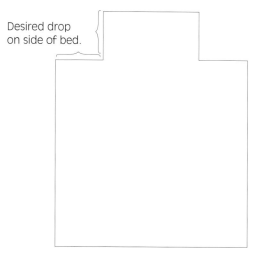

Desired drop
on side of bed.

Figure. 2–37
Cut out a square equal to the drop on the bed's side for a split corner.

Chapter 3

Finishing Touches

After the borders have been added, sometimes a small finishing touch adds that something extra to a quilt. It can be a piped insertion, an embroidered line, scalloped edges, Prairie Points, or a Dogtooth edge.

Shark's Teeth border, pattern on page 124.

Chapter 4

Gallery & Patterns

Full-size patterns and instructions are included for 17 different borders. They can be pieced or appliquéd, or both. Be sure to read the technical information supplied by the individual quilters. They have shared many tips and other information about how the quilts were constructed. There are finishing touches for each project, detailing some of the specific techniques used. The directions are written to fit the quilts pictured. You may need to change the sizes to fit your quilt.

The Patterns and the Quilters

Door County Christmas by Linda M. Roy, Corinth, Mississippi

Audrey II by Susan C. Derkacz, New Braunfels, Texas

Autumn Changes by Leslie Fehling, Waynesburg, Pennsylvania

Autumn Baskets by Shoko Ferguson, Clinton, Maryland

Twirling Stars by Shirley J. Stutz, Lore City, Ohio

Krokalia by Joan Haws, Anaheim, California

Beauty for Ashes by Loretta Coblentz, Sarasota, Florida

Dragonflowers by Suzanne Marshall, Clayton, Missouri

Margaret's Basket by Beatrice Walroth, Kingston, Ontario, Canada

Stop and Smell the Roses! by Tish Fiet, Jackson, Mississippi

Summer by Rita Ilene Ptacek, Downers Grove, Illinois

The Quilt for Kristen by Linda L. Brown, Duncanville, Texas

Eagle Medallion by Amy T. Chamberlin, Plano, Texas

Westford Sampler by Valerie R. Kelley, Pelham, New Hampshire

A Baltimore Adventure, Flora & Fauna by Ruth H. McIver, Johns Island, South Carolina

Door County Christmas

Door County Christmas was designed and hand quilted by Linda M. Roy and drafted and machine pieced by Dawn Shultz. The Darting Needles Quilt Guild, Menasha, WI, hand appliquéd 13 blocks, four outer diamond borders, and four corner units in border. This quilt was made for the guild's 1996 show raffle.

Audrey II

Audrey II by Susan C. Derkacz. Second-place winner in the Professional Appliqué category at the 1996 AQS Quilt Show. The borders use colors and shapes to repeat elements from the arcs in the center of the quilt.

Techniques
Rotary-cut half-square triangles
Machine piecing

For this sample border, the finished size of the pieced square is 3⅛".

1. Cut 4⅞" squares to end up with 4" squares to match blue squares
   12 purple
   6 yellow
   6 orange
2. Put right sides together
   6 purple and yellow
   6 purple and orange
3. Mark a diagonal line and sew a ¼" seam allowance on both sides of the line (Fig. 4–2).
   This makes 12 units. Cut apart on the drawn diagonal line and press open. You now have 24 half-square-triangle units.
4. Cut 23 blue 4" squares.
   Put a plain 4" blue square on top of a half-square-triangle unit, right sides together (Fig. 4–3, pg. 44). Mark the diagonal line (opposite the already sewn one) and sew ¼" on both sides of the line. Cut apart on the drawn diagonal line. You will have two mirror-image units.
5. To sew borders together, alternate yellow and orange units. The design can be a mirror image from the center of the border.
6. For the corner squares, cut 2 squares each of blue and yellow. Put right sides together. Mark a diagonal line

and sew ¼" on both sides of the line. Cut apart on the diagonal line.

To make half-square triangles in different sizes, use the following formula to cut your squares:

Half-square triangles — determine the finished size triangle you need and add ⅞" to the measurement of the short side (Fig. 4–2). The new measurement is the size square you need to cut. Example: The short side = 4" + ⅞" = 4⅞" square

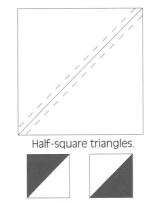

Half-square triangles.

Each set of two squares makes two half-square triangle squares.

Fig. 4–2
Making half-square triangles from squares.

Finishing touches
Susan made increments across the quilt even though the quilt was not quite symmetrical with the block; she used 11 squares on one half and 12 squares on the other. By mirroring the block, she has camouflaged the fact that the blocks reverse. Also, note the 1" purple single

band border she added between the quilt top and the border. That band is a good repeat of the single band used in the interior of the quilt, and it makes her center the correct size to fit the borders. Many interesting variations can be made using this same unit (Fig. 4–4).

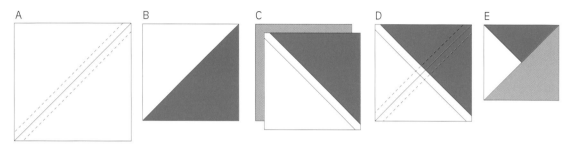

Figure 4–3
(A) Sew two squares together, ¼" on either side of diagonal line; (B) Cut A on diagonal line to make two B squares; (C) put B square on top of a plain square; (D) cut and sew opposite diagonal as before; (E) half-square triangle units (mirror images) result.

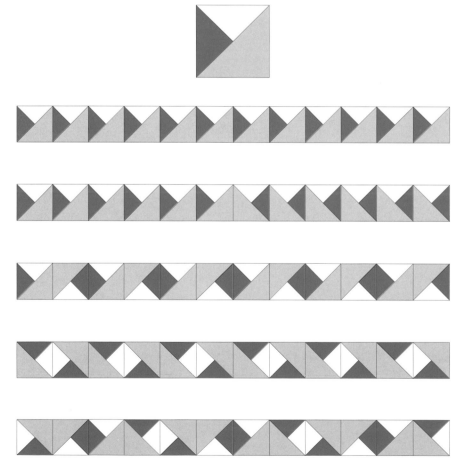

Figure 4–4
Variations made by rotating and mirroring the unit.

Autumn Changes

Autumn Changes by Leslie Fehling, 1995. Third-place winner in the Amateur Traditional Pieced category at the 1996 AQS Quilt Show.

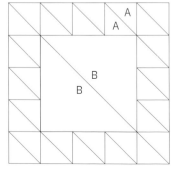

Technique

Machine pieced Lady of the Lake Blocks, 5" (finished)

The Lady of the Lake block from the center of the quilt was repeated in the border, using the red border fabric as the dark in every block for continuity. Leslie used the Electric Quilt 2.0 program to design her quilt. It gave her the ability to flip, rotate, move, and recolor the blocks at the touch of a button. She tried several border variations, some very elaborate. In the end, she chose the simplest one because it enhances the central design without competing with it. Sometimes simplicity is the best choice. Blocks are set on point, with half-square triangles to complete the edge of the border.

1. Make the number of Lady of the Lake blocks you need for your quilt. Use the piecing templates on this page.

2. Cut an 8½" square diagonally in both directions to make 4 side triangles. Cut 8" square in half diagonally to make 2 corner triangles. These corner and side triangles are generously sized and will need to be trimmed after border is assembled. Make the number of triangles you need for your quilt.

3. A 3½"-wide (finished) single-band border can be added after the pieced border to finish the edge of the quilt.

Finishing touches

This is a good example of using the same pieced block in the center of the quilt and in the borders. Only the colors have been changed.

Block Piecing

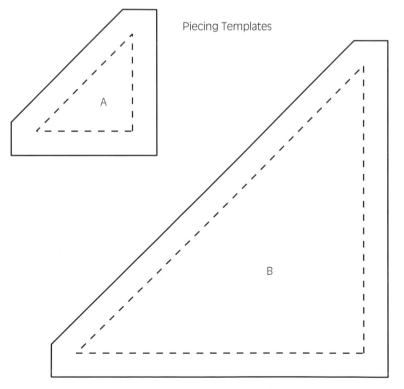

Piecing Templates

Autumn Baskets

Autumn Baskets by Shoko Ferguson, 1995. Scrap fabrics are used in a variation of the Delectable Mountains pattern. The scraps are colorful, but very busy, so only two colors are used for the outside border.

F

B

D

E

Twirling Stars

Twirling Stars by Shirley Stutz, 1995. The quilt design and coloration of Twirling Stars were the inspiration for this border. Twirling Stars has nine different borders in a 12" span. A border print serves as the theme fabric, and three different elements from this fabric are used in the borders.

Krokalia

Krokalia by Joan Haws, 1995. This pattern was inspired by a book on Greek architecture. Krokalia is a decorative mosaic of pebbles found traditionally in homes and courtyards in the Dodencanese Islands.

Borders & Finishing Touches

Krokalia

Techniques
Hand appliqué
Continuous bias strips

1. Cut 1" continuous bias strips and use bias bars to make ¼" finished bias strips. Approximately four yards of the navy blue print was used in this quilt.
2. Use saucers to space and shape the swirls to fit the borders. Make master paper patterns for the borders.
3. Cut the borders the correct size and trace a single line of the design on the fabric for placement of the bias strips.
4. Use your favorite method to appliqué the bias strips in place. Remember to stitch the insides of the curves first, then stitch the outside edges of the curves.
5. A continuous bias strip is used in each corner.
6. Make templates for the petals from freezer paper for both right- and left-

hand petals. Iron the freezer paper templates to the wrong side of the fabric. Cut out the petals, adding ¼" turn-under allowances by eye as you cut. Press the allowances over the template edge with an iron. Peel off the freezer paper. The edge is ready to be appliquéd.

Joan used Nancy Pearson's twisted fabric technique to join the petals to the end of the bias strips.

Finishing touches
The blue inner border provides a good frame around the design in the center. See how increasing the size of the design in the border allows you to notice both the center and the borders of the quilt.

Variations: This scroll design can easily be adapted in a variety of ways. Figure 4–6 shows staggered and half-staggered scrolls, S-scrolls, double S-scrolls, and a vine scroll.

Figure 4–6
Variations of scroll designs.

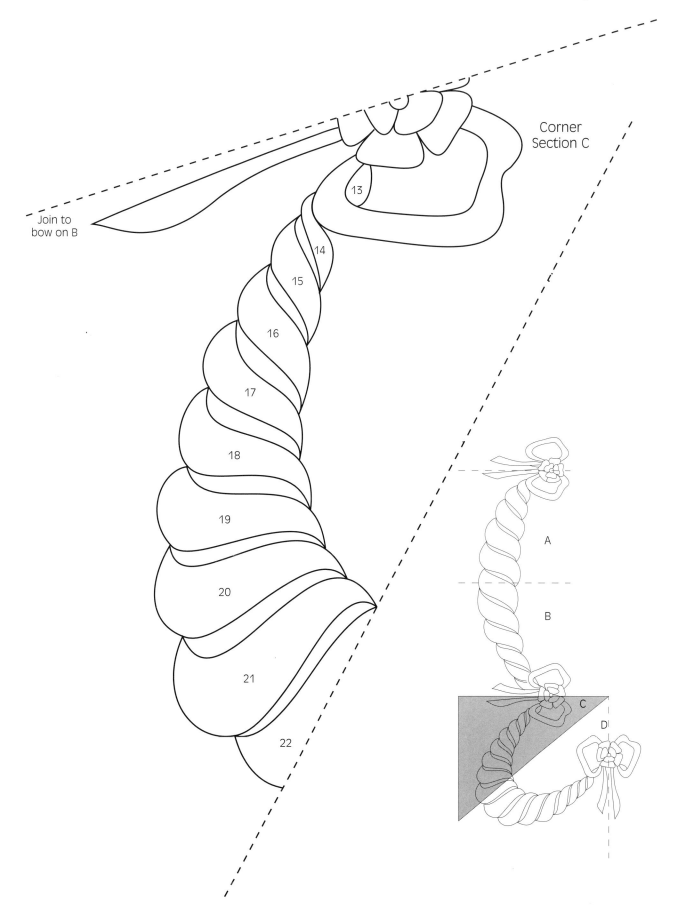

Corner
Section C

Join to
bow on B

13

14

15

16

17

18

19

20

21

22

A

B

C

D

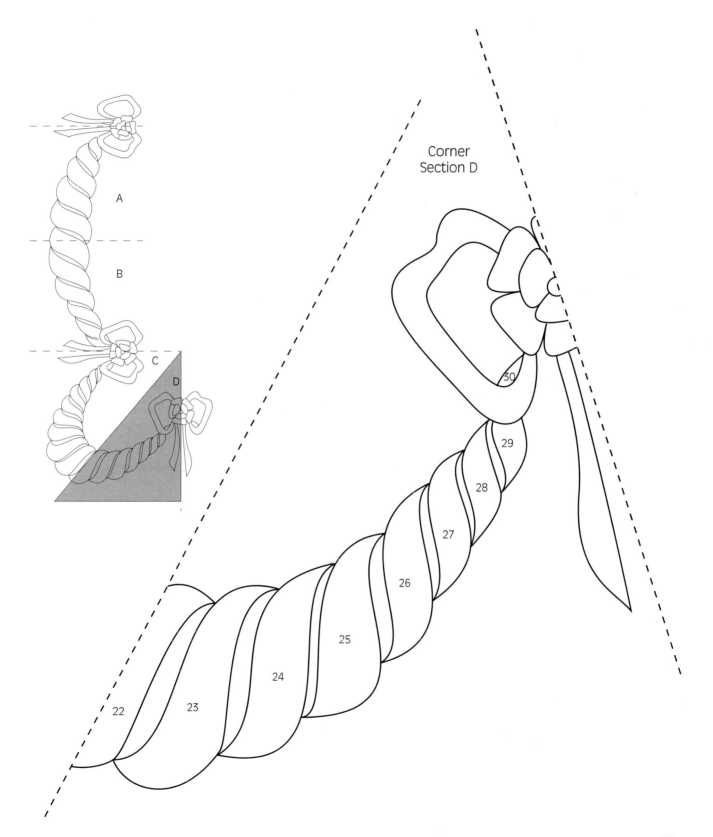

Corner
Section D

Dragonflowers

Dragonflowers by Suzanne Marshall, 1994. The curving lines of the borders are designed to accent the free-flowing flowers, so characteristic of Art Nouveau. The maker was influenced to devise the swirling black borders by designs in *Frames and Decorations of the Art Nouveau Period*, a Dover publication.

Dragonflowers

Technique
Hand appliqué

1. Cut the borders to fit the sides of the quilt.
2. Make a paper template of the border design. If you need to adjust the design to fit your quilt, adjustments can be made at the center point of a side, or any of the flowing elements can be shortened or lengthened to make it fit.
3. Use your favorite method to appliqué the design to the background fabric.

Finishing touches
Suzanne has used design repeats effectively. A small-scale dark border surrounds the central design, and a similar, larger version makes up the outer border.

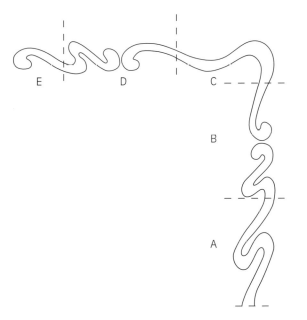

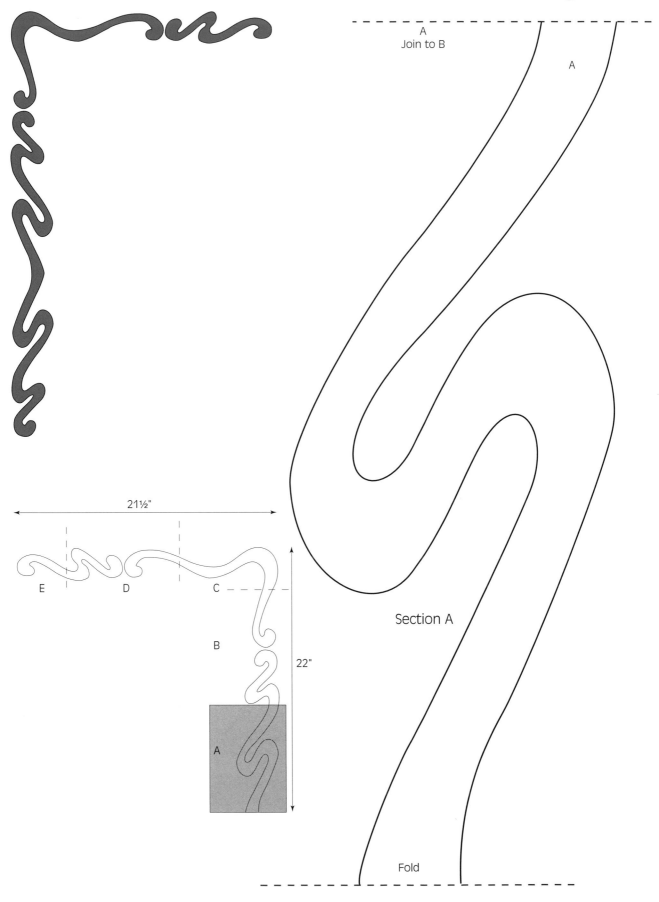

A
Join to B

A

21½"

E   D   C

B

22"

A

Section A

Fold

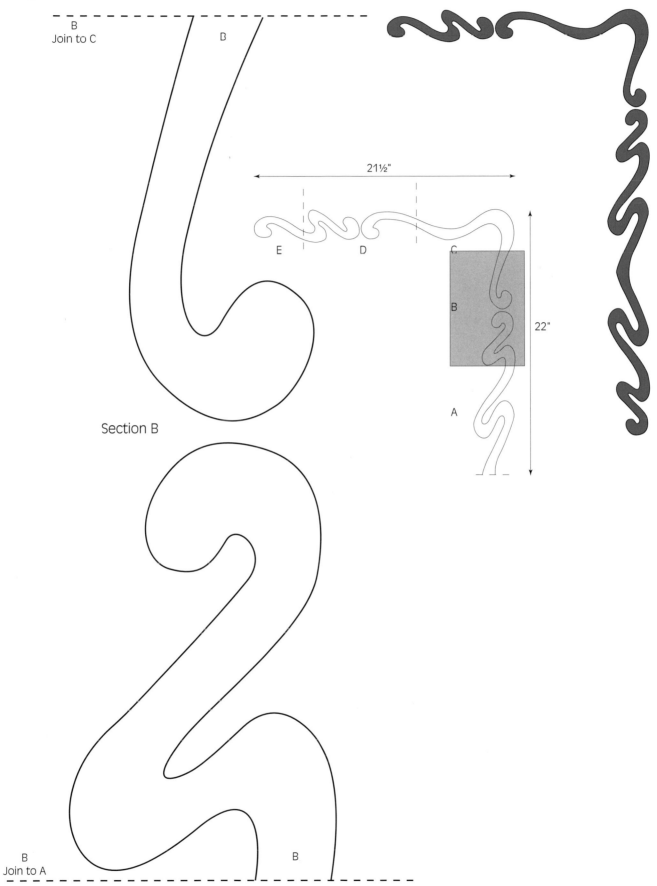

B
Join to C

B

21½"

E   D   C

B   22"

A

Section B

B

B
Join to A

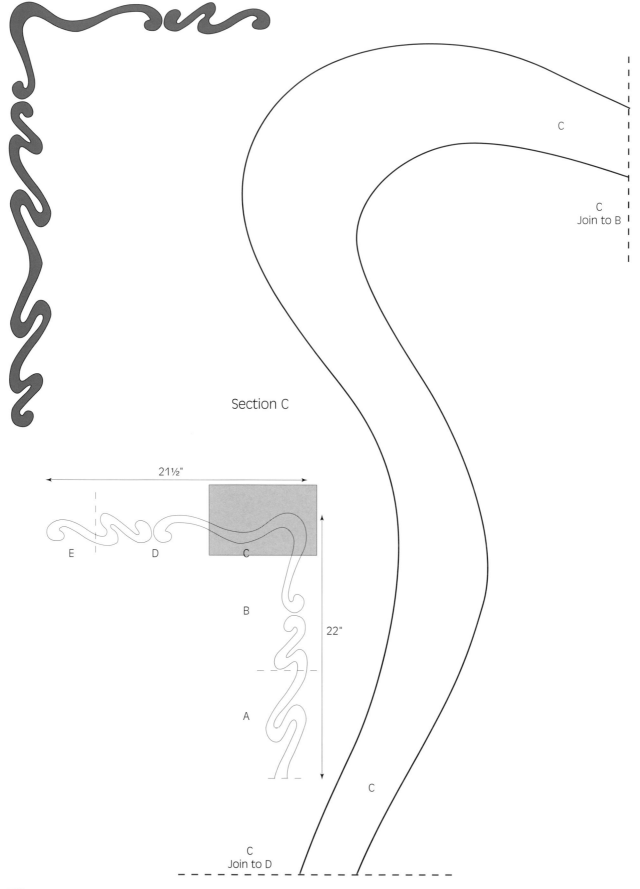

Section C

21½"

E   D   C

B

22"

A

C
Join to D

C

C
Join to B

Dragonflowers

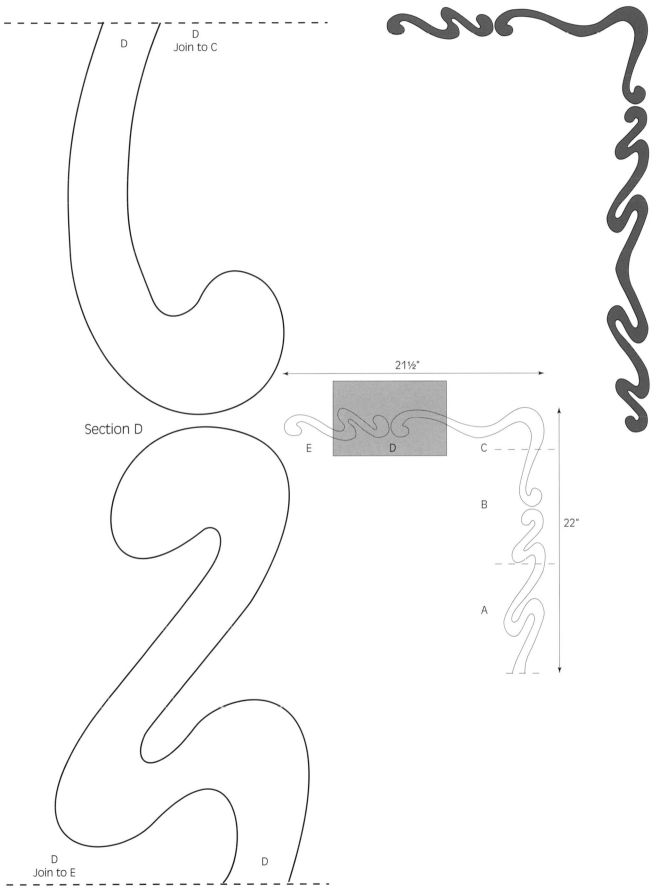

D

D
Join to C

Section D

21½"

E   D   C

B

22"

A

D
Join to E

D

Borders & Finishing Touches

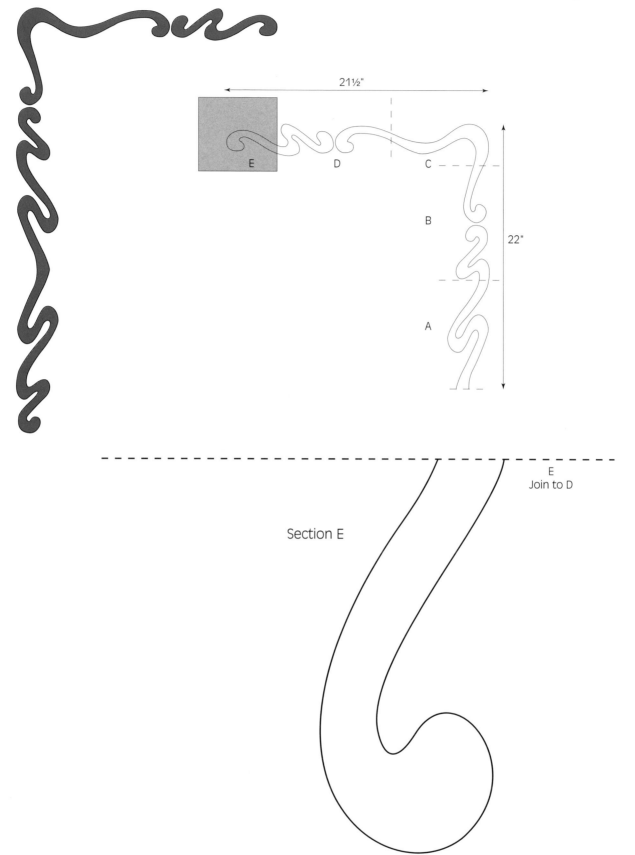

21½"

22"

E

D

C

B

A

E
Join to D

Section E

Margaret's Basket

Margaret's Basket by Beatrice Walroth for the Kingston Heirloom Quilters, 1994. When the basket blocks were finished and sewn together, the Kingston Heirloom Quilters realized this quilt deserved a special border. The dusty rose accent fabric is used as a narrow single-band border separating the borders from the center of the quilt. It is also used to give dimension to the glazed cotton triple bows that reflect the shape of the basket handles.

Techniques
Hand appliqué
Prairie Points

1. Refer to the photo for placement of light and dark fabrics. Make templates for each piece; then number pattern pieces in stitching order and identify which fabric is to be used in each one. Two copies of the pattern can be drawn, one for reference and one for cutting the pattern pieces.

2. Cut out the individual pieces in fabric, leaving the patterns attached. Lay out the pieces on a strip of flannel cut to the width of the border. This holds them in place where they can remain undisturbed. Roll the flannel around an empty aluminum foil core for storage.

3. Join the first three segments of the trailing ribbons. Thimble or finger pressing the seams open. Turn under and baste the allowances as if it were one piece. Replace this unit on the flannel. Next, pair by pair, assemble the bow units. Baste the seam allowances as above. Continue in this

manner until all the units are joined, except the knot. It is left until after the bow has been applied to the border to allow for slight adjustments.

4. The corner bows are assembled in half units. These units are then applied with the pieces that overlap the miter.

5. Trim away the underside where the ribbons overlap one another or the vine to reduce the thickness of the vine beneath the ribbon's edge.

6. Before applying the ribbons and bows to the border, mark the areas that must be left open for the vine to slip under.

7. Prairie Points and piping are stitched to the edges of the border. A ⅜" finished double, bias binding is applied to complete the quilt (Fig. 4–7).

Finishing touches
A new color can be successfully introduced into the border area. The single narrow-band border of dusty rose around the center of the quilt ties the color to the outer border with a small amount of the same color used in the bows.

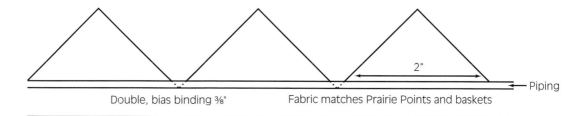

Double, bias binding ⅜"   Fabric matches Prairie Points and baskets
2"
Piping

Figure 4–7
Prairie Points and piping on edges of quilt.

Margaret's Basket

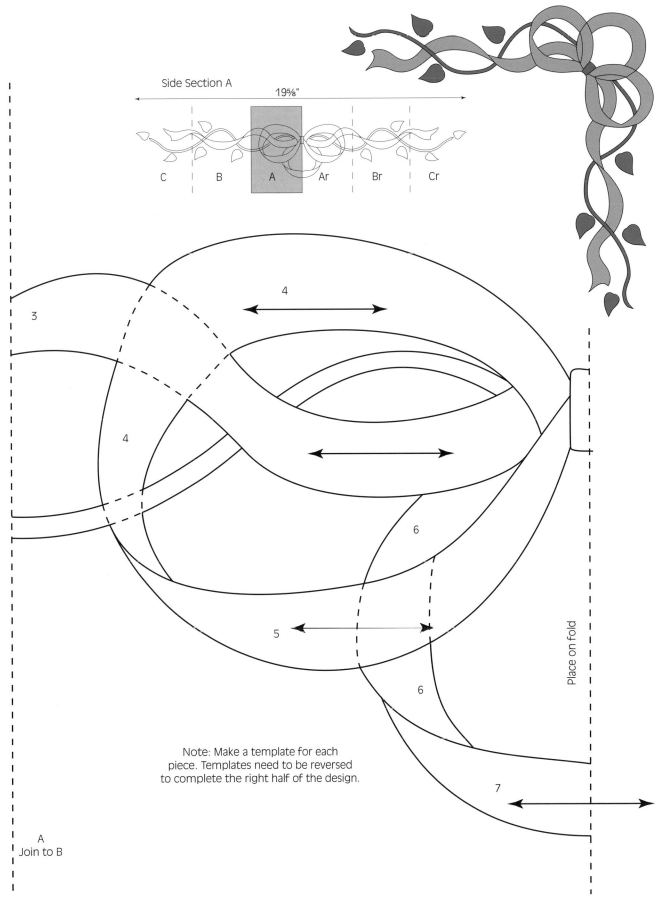

Side Section A

19⅝"

C   B   A   Ar   Br   Cr

3

4

4

6

5

6

7

Place on fold

Note: Make a template for each
piece. Templates need to be reversed
to complete the right half of the design.

A
Join to B

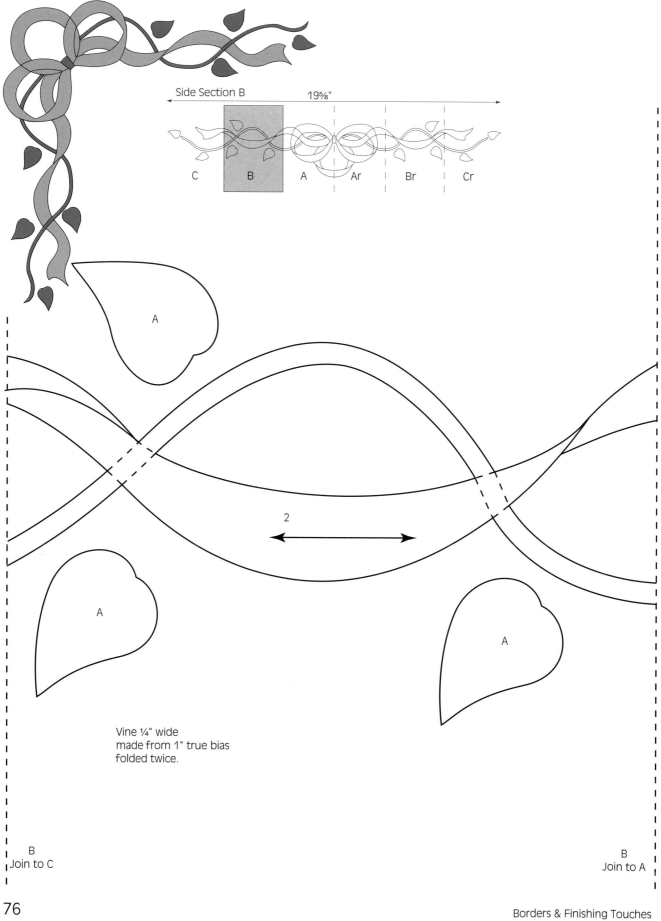

Side Section B

19⅝"

C   B   A   Ar   Br   Cr

A

A

2

A

Vine ¼" wide
made from 1" true bias
folded twice.

B
Join to C

B
Join to A

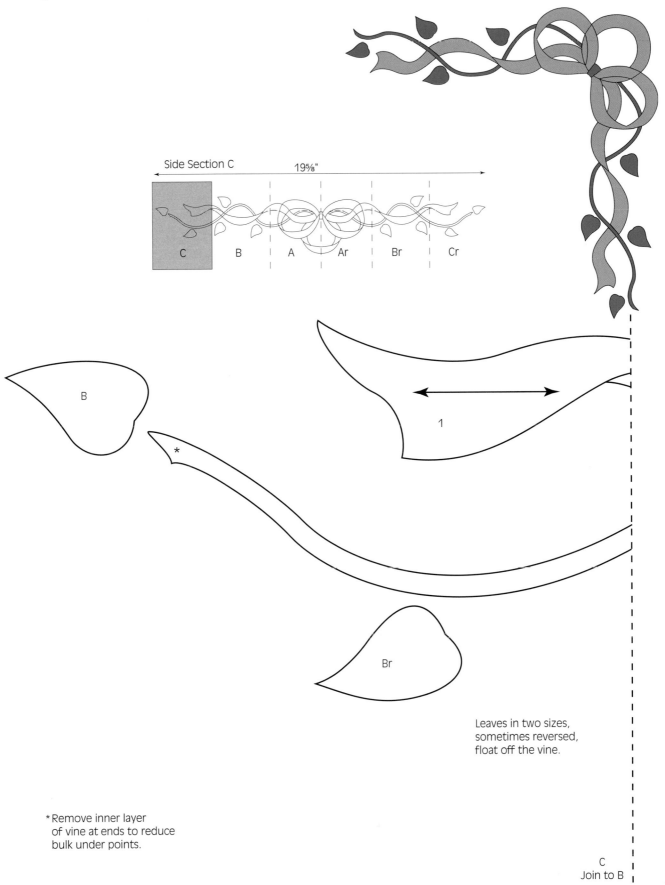

Side Section C

19⅝"

C   B   A   Ar   Br   Cr

B

*

1

Br

Leaves in two sizes,
sometimes reversed,
float off the vine.

* Remove inner layer
of vine at ends to reduce
bulk under points.

C
Join to B

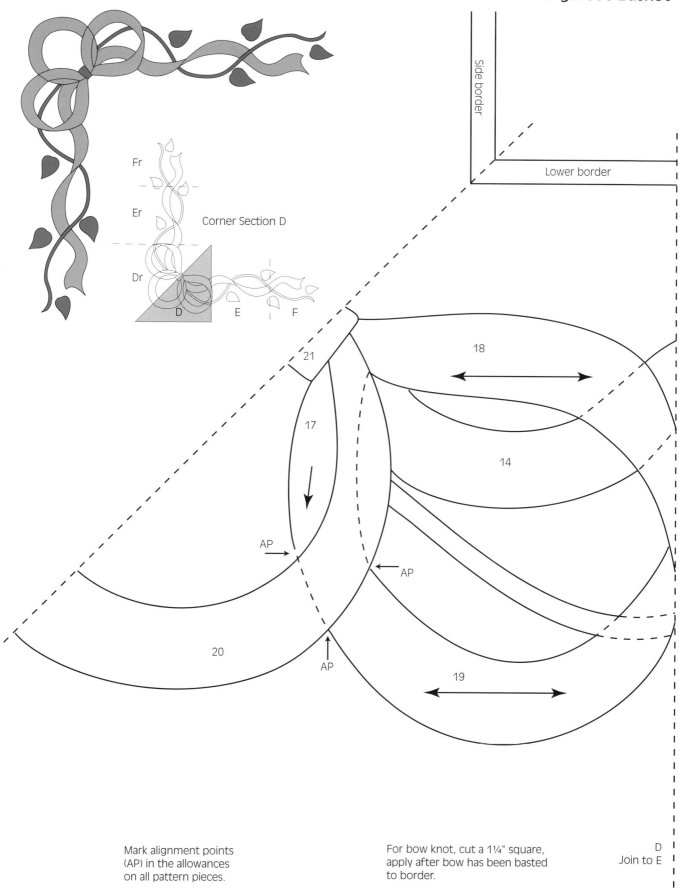

Fr

Er

Corner Section D

Dr

D   E   F

Side border

Lower border

18

21

17

14

AP →

← AP

AP

20

↑ AP

19

Mark alignment points
(AP) in the allowances
on all pattern pieces.

For bow knot, cut a 1¼" square,
apply after bow has been basted
to border.

D
Join to E

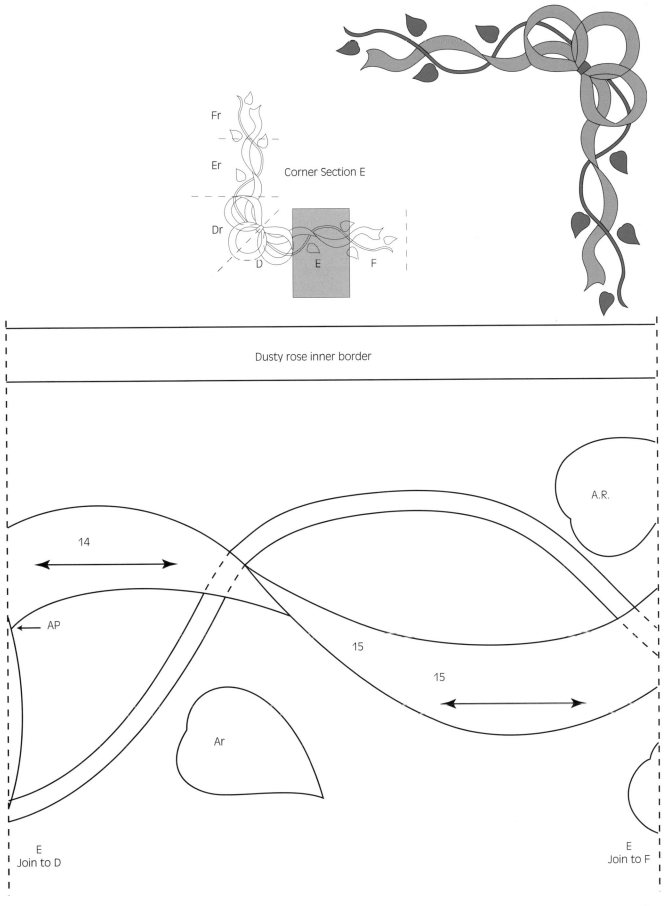

Fr

Er

Dr

Corner Section E

D   E   F

Dusty rose inner border

A.R.

14

AP

15

15

Ar

E
Join to D

E
Join to F

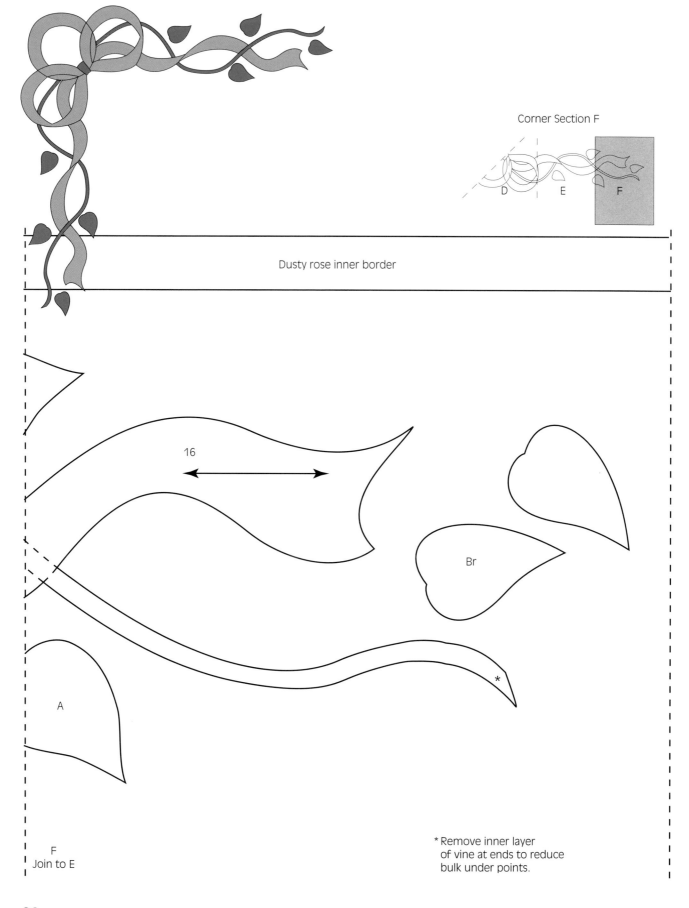

Margaret's Basket

Corner Section F

D   E   F

Dusty rose inner border

16

Br

A

F
Join to E

* Remove inner layer
of vine at ends to reduce
bulk under points.

80

Borders & Finishing Touches

Stop and Smell the Roses!

Stop and Smell the Roses! by Tish Fiet, 1996. Roses have always been a favorite of this maker, so when she began planning the border, a design of roses and buds amid curving vines and leaves seemed to be a natural complement to the collection of rose blocks.

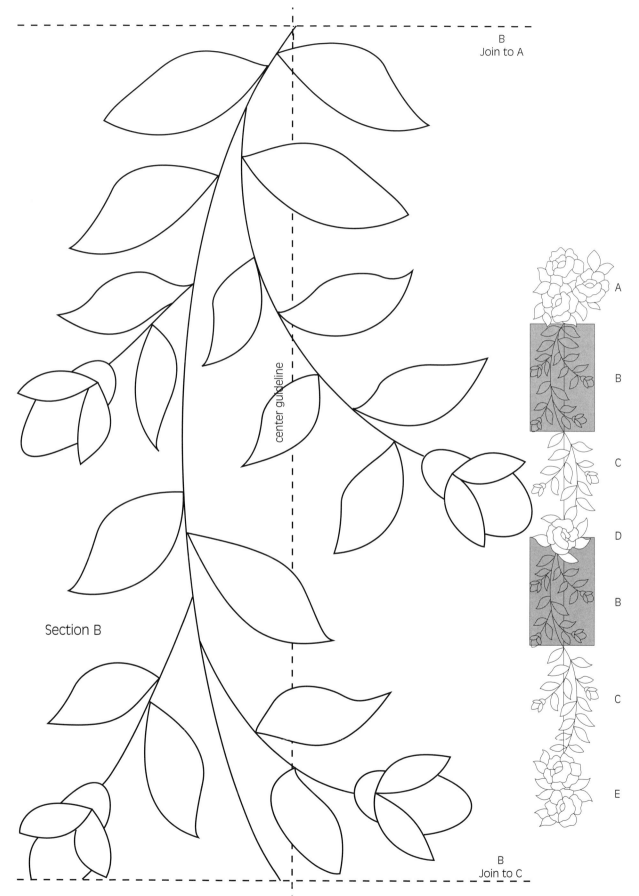

Stop and Smell the Roses!

B
Join to A

center guideline

Section B

A

B

C

D

B

C

E

B
Join to C

84

Borders & Finishing Touches

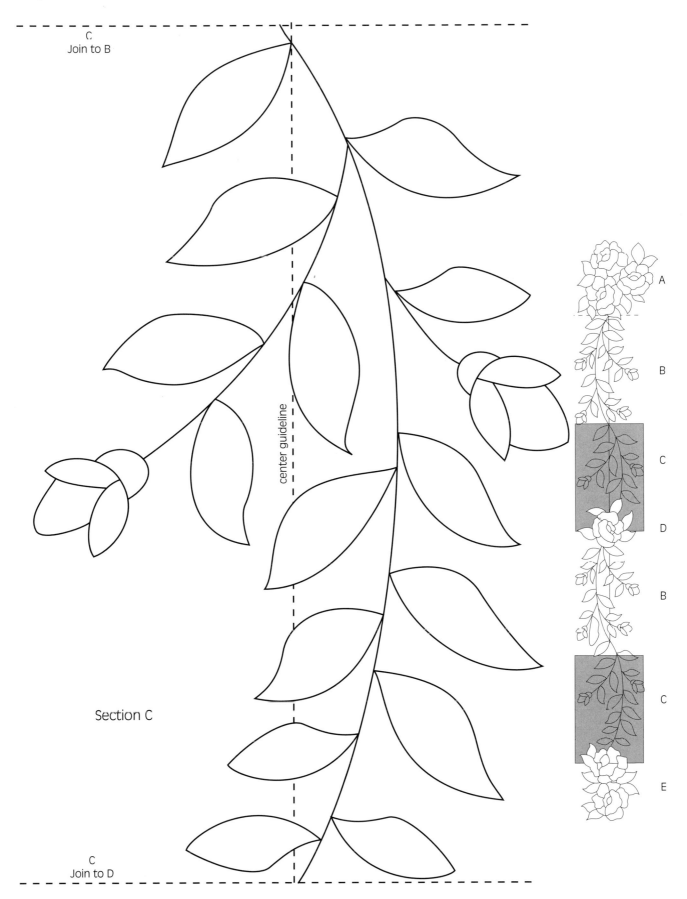

C
Join to B

center guideline

Section C

C
Join to D

A

B

C

D

B

C

E

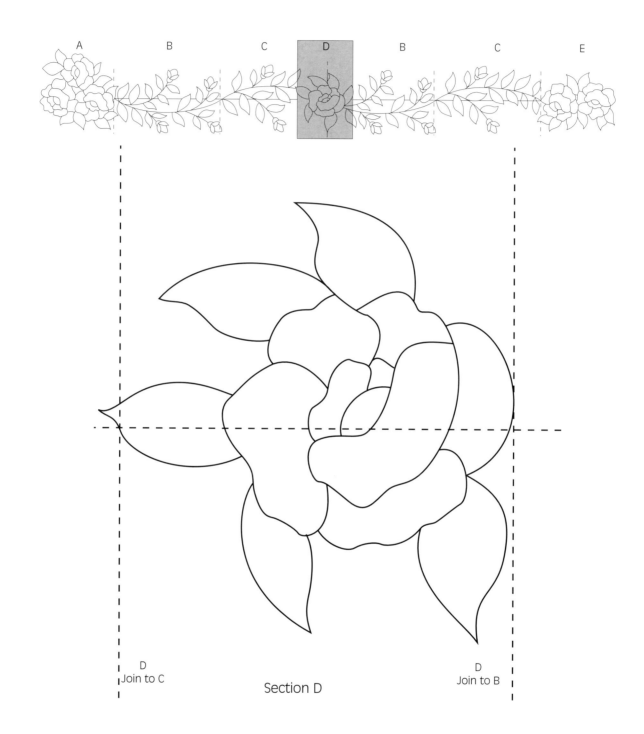

A   B   C   D   B   C   E

D
Join to C

D
Join to B

Section D

Stop and Smell the Roses!

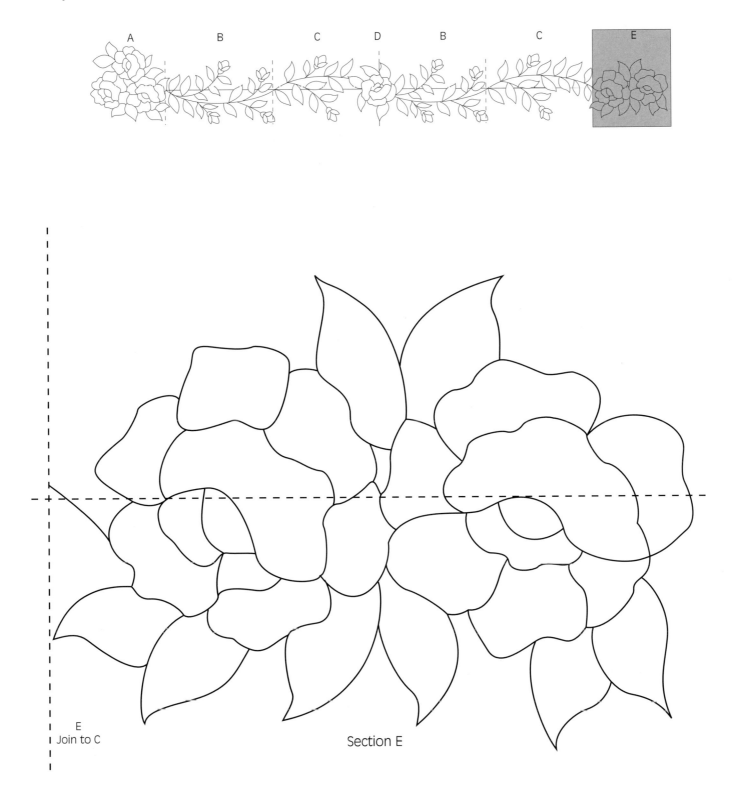

E
Join to C

Section E

Summer

Summer by Rita Ilene Ptacek, 1995. After the center of this quilt was machine pieced, the border was added to make it larger. Different yellow fabrics give sparkle to the quilt in the border and center. The background fabric, with tiny yellow stars, is a good color to complement the other yellow fabrics.

Techniques
Needle-turn appliqué
Bias strips for vines and stems

1. Determine the length of arc needed for the vine to fit your border. (see Making the Borders Fit, page 22).
2. Cut borders to fit your quilt and needle turn appliqué the grapevine (½" bias strips) in place first.
3. Position the stems (⅜" bias strips) and the sunflowers, balancing each side with the same number of flowers. A variety of fabrics is used for the vines and stems. The sunflower design is a single repeat. The flowers are reversed every other design unit along the length of the border. If you need to make any adjustments for your quilt, flowers can be added or subtracted or, for minor adjustments, try lengthening or shortening the stems.
4. Add grapes (three colors of purple are used here) and grape leaves where wanted.
5. Use the grapes and different leaves to fill any empty spaces. The grapes range from dark color values inside to light values on the outside of the clusters.

Rita used a sunflower design from *The Easy Art of Applique* by Mimi Dietrich and Roxi Eppler, and leaf patterns by Muriel Douglas, Jean Wells, and Laurene Sinema. Since all of these copyrighted designs are printed in other books, the patterns provided here are new designs drawn by the author, who used real flowers and leaves. The results will be similar but not exactly like those used in Rita's quilt.

Finishing touches
Repeating colors, especially the bright yellows, from the center of the quilt to the borders ties the two parts together.

Experiment with flowers, leaves, and fruit to design your own border.

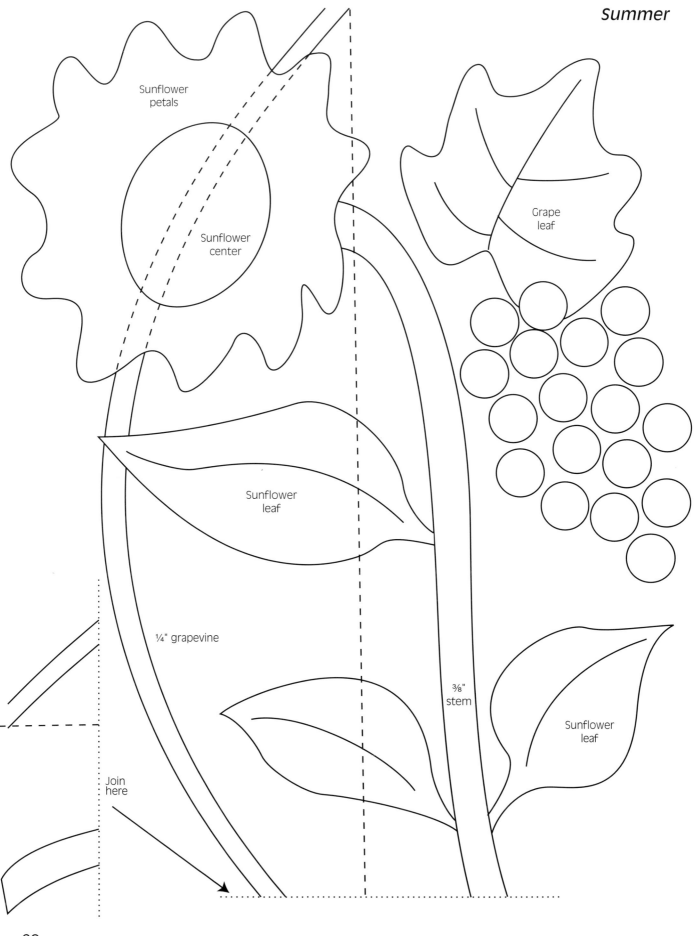

Sunflower
petals

Sunflower
center

Grape
leaf

Sunflower
leaf

¼" grapevine

⅜"
stem

Sunflower
leaf

Join
here

The Quilt for Kristen

The Quilt for Kristen by Linda L. Brown, 1995. Second place in the Amateur Appliqué category at the 1996 AQS Quilt Show.

The inspiration for this quilt came from watercolor illustrations found in *Treasury of Flower Fairies* by Cicely Mary Barker. The overall design is similar to those found in oriental rugs. Skydyes, the hand-painted cottons by Mickey Lawler, helped foster Linda's creativity. Books and articles by Nancy Pearson, Jeana Kimball, and Elly Sienkiewicz supplied the necessary knowledge Linda needed to tackle her first attempt at designing an appliqué quilt from scratch.

Techniques
Needle-turn, reverse, and layered
      appliqué
Embroidery

1. Fabric requirements 78" x 92" quilt:
    Main background color (cream) and blue
        2¾ yds. each of cream and blue
        1⅛ yds. white
2. Cut fabric as follows:
    Cream:
    Two strips ⅞" x 92"
    Two strips ⅞" x 78"
    Two strips 3¾" x 92"
    Two strips 3¾" x 78"
    Blue:
    Four strips 6½" x 46¼"
    Four strips 6½" x 39¼"
    Four strips ⅞" x 92"
    Four strips ⅞" x 78"
    White:
    Eight 11" squares
    For appliqué flowers and leaves: Cut ¼-yd. pieces of several colors in lights, mediums, and darks, including many greens (up to ½ yd. of some

fabrics, especially greens).

3. In choosing colors, check to see that no one flower, border, or design detracts from the rest. The background color should complement the appliqué, not fight for attention. Values are very important. Often, a single flower may contain as many as eight different fabrics. Include lights, mediums, and darks in the quilt, but not in equal amounts. Keep in mind that a fabric may take on a different value when placed on a colored background instead of on a white background. Use the same general colors in the border that are used in the quilt center. If one color pops out visually, chances are there is too great a contrast between it and its neighbor. Or, you may have used too little of that stand-out color. Sometimes more appears to be less. If you run out of a fabric, use another that is similar in color and value.

4. Use pre-washed 100% cotton fabrics, perhaps some hand dyed, and a good quality 50–60-weight cotton thread for appliqué. Use the same shade of thread as your appliqué piece or a shade slightly darker. Linda prefers using a long thin milliner's needle, and she marks with a sharp pencil or a white Berol Prismacolor pencil.

5. Store templates along with cut out appliqué pieces in small baggies. The appliqué pieces are made by tracing around the templates on the right side of the fabric. To reverse a

design, reverse the template when tracing your appliqué pieces. Add ⅛"–³⁄₁₆" turn-under allowances as you cut. Your thin pencil line is the sewing line. and it will be completely covered if a blind stitch is used for appliquéing. Use small, close stitches.

6. Linda prefers not to mark the design onto the background. She simply places a see-through pattern over the background fabric and slips the piece in the appropriate place, pinning it to the background. Or, you can choose to transfer the design to the background fabric by using a light box, sunny window, or a light under a glass table. You must be sure you cut out your templates and fabric pieces very accurately so you can cover all of the pencil marks on the background. (Marking slightly inside the edges of the appliqué pieces can give you a little fudge factor if you choose to mark the background.) If any marks show on the background, remove them before you press the appliquéd piece.

7. Check your quilt top size and adjust any border measurements before cutting the border strips.

8. Since the raw edges of the border fabrics could fray during appliquéing, cut the blue borders a little longer and wider than indicated. This will also allow you to trim and square up the appliquéd piece to the correct size before adding the border strips on either side.

9. You may want to embroider, rather than appliqué, small details on the quilt center and borders.

10. Linda usually prefers not to cut away the background fabrics, but sometimes the extra bulk needs to be removed in the layered appliqué in this quilt. You can partially appliqué an overlapping piece, lift it up, and carefully trim away the excess (stem, etc.) underneath. If it looks okay, feels okay, and you don't have to quilt through it, leave it. Otherwise, trim it.

11. Border assembly: Appliqué blue border strips, leaving the side medallions for later. Sew the appropriate blue strips together, end to end. Add the narrow cream and blue border strips to both sides of all four borders and add the 3¾"-wide cream strips to the outside edges. Press all seam allowances away from the blue border. (Be sure to remove any visible pencil marks before pressing.)

12. Side Medallions – Method 1: Make a paper template for the white medallion insert, using the dash lines on patterns A and B, pages 95 and 96, as guides. Center the template on the right side of one of the 11" squares and draw around it. Add ¼" allowances by eye as you cut out the insert. Position the cut-out white insert on the center of a joined border strip, using the pattern as a placement guide. Pin in place and machine stitch on the drawn line. Turn to the wrong side. You need to have only one background layer, so

carefully cut away the blue fabric in the center of the medallion, leaving a ¼" allowance.

Method 2: After tracing the medallion onto the white square, do not cut it out. Instead, position the whole square on the center of the border strip, pin, and stitch in place. Trim away excess fabric, leaving a ¼" allowance. You are less likely to distort the shape of the medallion using this method when stitching.

Add the appliqué to the medallion, except for pieces 28 and 29. Take care to cover all raw edges with the appliqué.

13. Sew one of the borders to the quilt top, but leave the mitering for later. Appliqué pieces 28 and 29. Repeat with remaining three border sections. Miter all four corners. (You will have excess bulk where seams meet, but this can be trimmed away after you sew on the medallion.)

14. Corner Medallions: Place the white inserts for the four corner medallions on the bias to follow the grain line of the rest of the quilt.

Take the remaining four white squares and fold each one in half, corner to opposite corner, to make a triangle. Press the fold. Proceed as you did for the side medallions, except this time position the pattern on the pressed diagonal lines on the white squares.

15. Quilting suggestions: Quilt around each appliqué piece. Echo quilt the rest of the blue border. Use a grid design in the white areas. Stitch in the ditch on narrow strips.

Finishing touches

The borders of this quilt are recommended for intermediate to advanced quilters. Appliquéing on top of the multiple bands beautifully showcases the flowers and makes a grand finishing edge.

Side Medallion A

stitching & template line

A
Join to B

Side Medallion B

B
Join to A

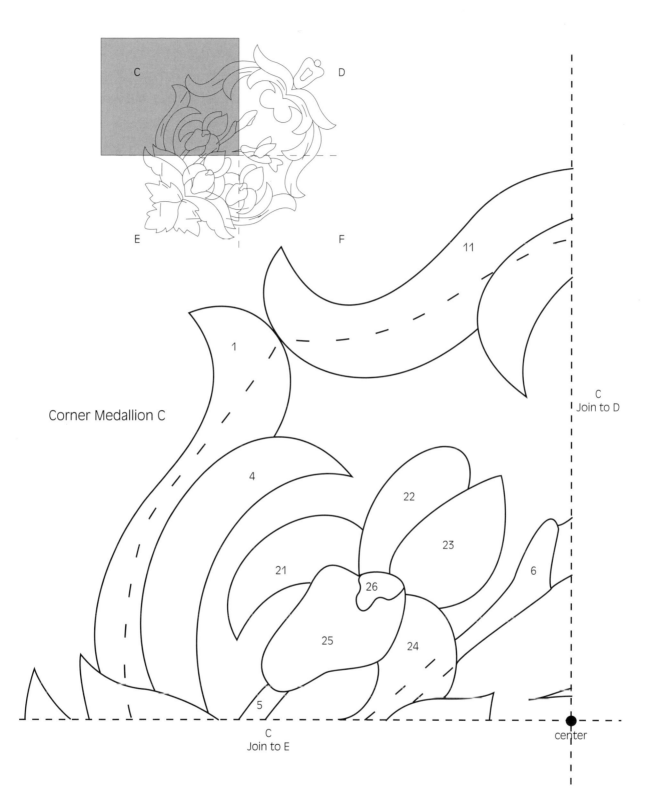

C

D

E

F

Corner Medallion C

C
Join to D

C
Join to E

center

11

1

4

22

23

21

6

26

25

24

5

C

D

E

F

17

18

15

14

16

Corner Medallioin D

D
Join to C

13

20

19

42

41

43

center

D
Join to F

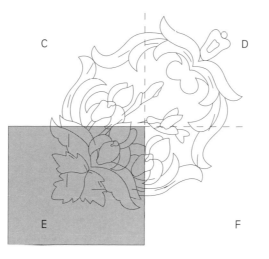

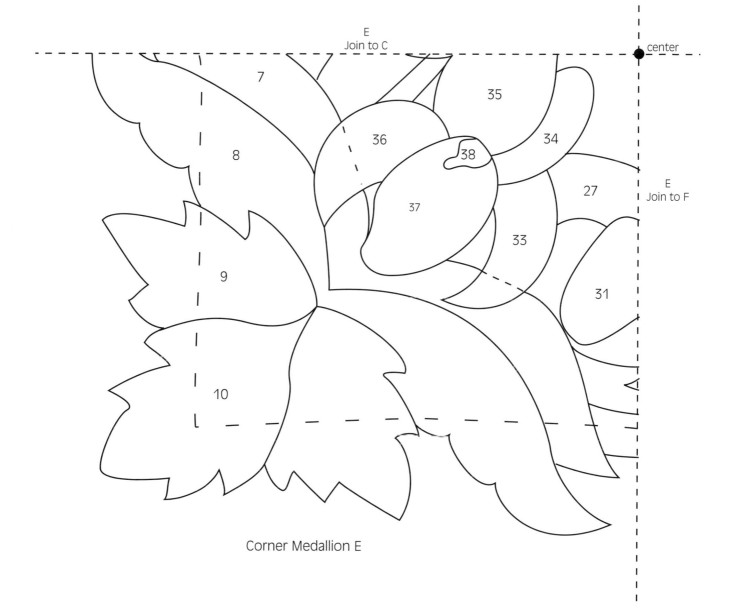

Corner Medallion E

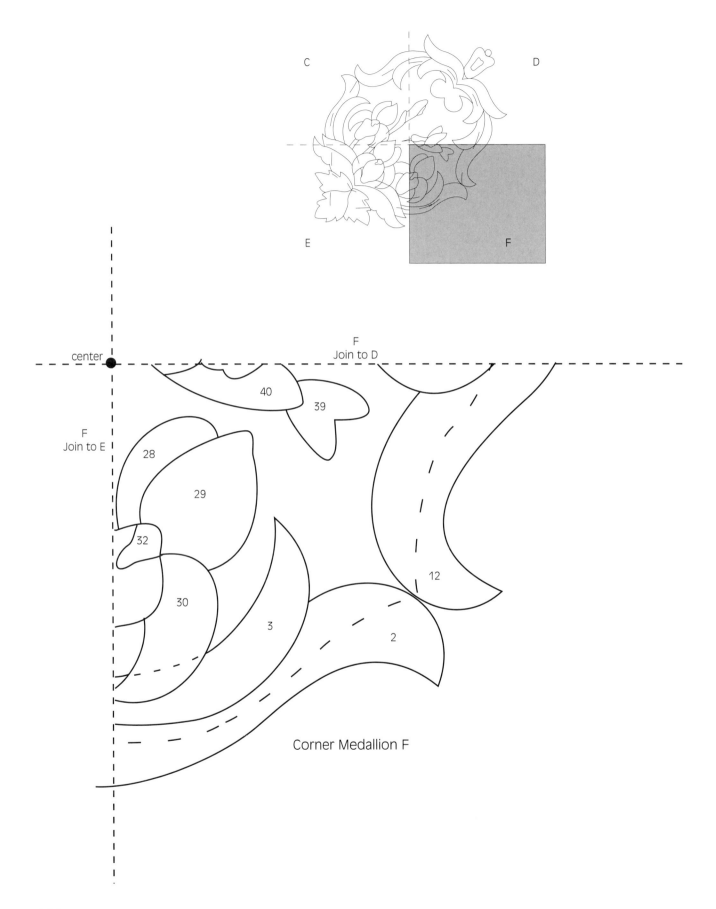

Corner Medallion F

G

17¾"

Section G

G
Join to H

H
Join to G

Section H

17¾"

H

Eagle Medallion

Eagle Medallion by Amy Chamberlin, 1995. Four different borders were added to enlarge this medallion-style quilt. The eagle is surrounded by a scalloped circle, followed by waves, vines, and finally, the swag and tassel border.

Techniques
Machine appliqué
Trapunto

Border A: (Scalloped circle)
1. Determine the size of one swag to fit your border (see Making the Border Fit, page 22). Make any necessary adjustments in the center of the swag.
2. Cut templates from freezer paper.
3. Press the shiny side of freezer paper templates to the wrong side of fabric.
4. Cut out pieces, adding ¼" turn-under allowances.
5. Stitch the two sections of the swag together.
6. Allowances are turned under on both inner and outer edges and secured with glue stick to the paper side of freezer paper.
7. Use a narrow zigzag to machine appliqué with the sewing foot on and feed dogs engaged.
8. The tassels between the swags are also prepared over freezer paper and machine appliquéd in place. Stuff the tassels from the back by making a slit in the background fabric.

Quilting
Mark quilting lines with a blue wash-out marker. Test marker before using it on your quilt to make sure it will wash out. When finished, the quilt can be put through a full cold-water cycle in a commercial machine at a self-service laundry. Two cotton threads of the same color can be used with a #90 machine-quilting needle when a darker line is desired. In the stipple quilting, use one strand of cotton thread. In the darker stitching areas within the scalloped circle, #50 machine-embroidery thread is used. Six strands of embroidery floss is woven in the quilting stitches around the inner and outer edges of the scalloped circle, as well as the outer edge of the waves to produce stronger lines.

Finishing touches
Using the tan fabric in four distinctly different styles of borders creates an overall pleasing design. These borders would be equally beautiful if they were used individually.

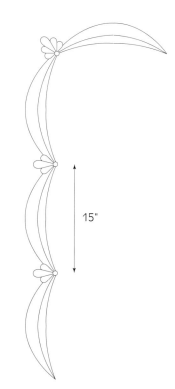

15"

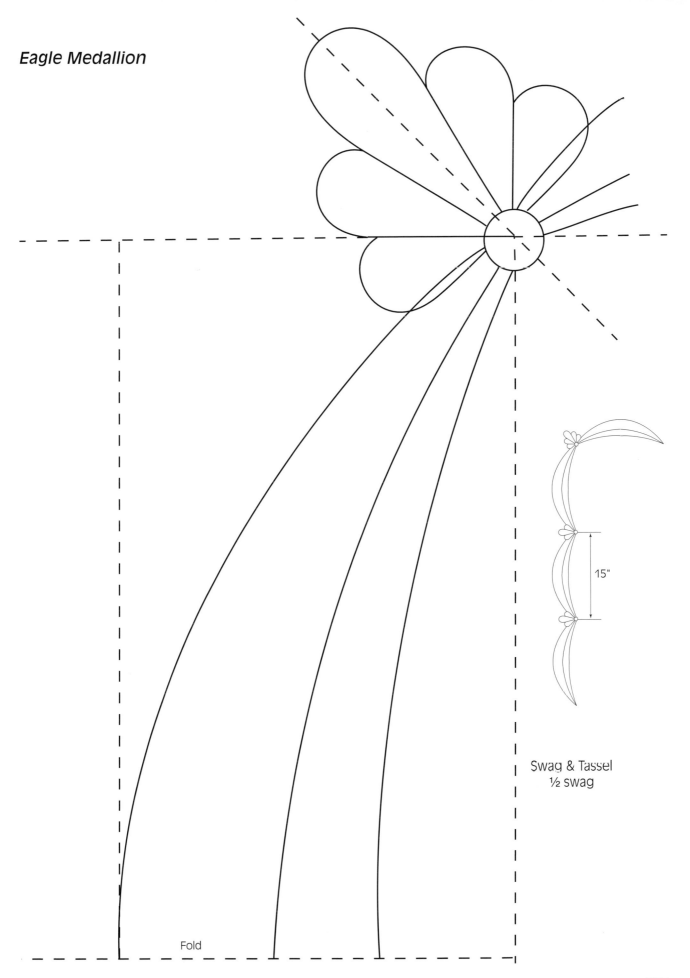

15"

Swag & Tassel
½ swag

Fold

Westford Sampler

Westford Sampler by Valerie R. Kelley, 1995. Third place, Theme Wall Quilt: Flowers, Professional or Amateur, 1996 AQS Quilt Show. This quilt was inspired by a cabbage rose print. The body of the quilt was finished before the border was designed. Originally, Valerie had planned to use the cabbage rose print in the border, but it did not work. Instead, she used the cabbage rose print on the back of the quilt.

Borders & Finishing Touches

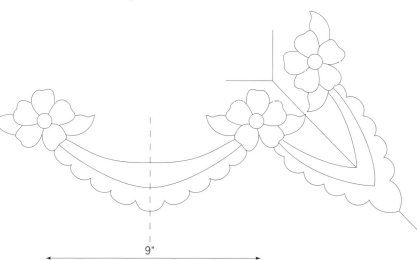

Techniques

Freezer paper appliqué
Embroidery: blanket, fly, and
   stem stitches

1. Determine the size of the swags to fit your quilt. If the swag needs to be adjusted, shorten it in the center. If less than a full scallop is removed, the scallops will need to be adjusted as well. The swag can be lengthened by adding additional scallops.

2. Make templates for the two swag sections. Cut the scallop from one fabric and the top section from a second fabric. The scallops could also be cut as a single unit in one fabric.

3. Make templates for the flower petal, center, and leaf. Note that one leaf is reversed in each flower unit.

4. Make templates for the corner unit.

5. Cut 6½" wide border strips to fit your quilt.

6. Appliqué and embroider the swags to the border sections before sewing the borders to the center. After the borders have been stitched to the quilt and the corners mitered, appliqué the corner motifs.

7. To form the Dogtooth edge of the quilt, cut the binding 1½" wide (see page 37 for Dogtooth directions). Sew the binding to the back of the quilt (usually the binding is sewn to the front first), with the right sides together, using a ¼" seam allowance. Fold the binding to the front of the quilt. Valerie quilted the border with 1" lines. This made a marker for her to clip the binding in 1" increments to form the Dogtooth edge. The edges of the Dogtooth are appliquéd in place. The Dogtooth edges can be quilted.

Finishing touches

Notice how the swags are spaced the same as the blocks in the center of the quilt. The corner motifs fit the imaginary square in the corners of the quilt. Valerie used a clever method for binding the quilt and adding the decorative Dogtooth border, all in one operation.

9"

9"

Fold

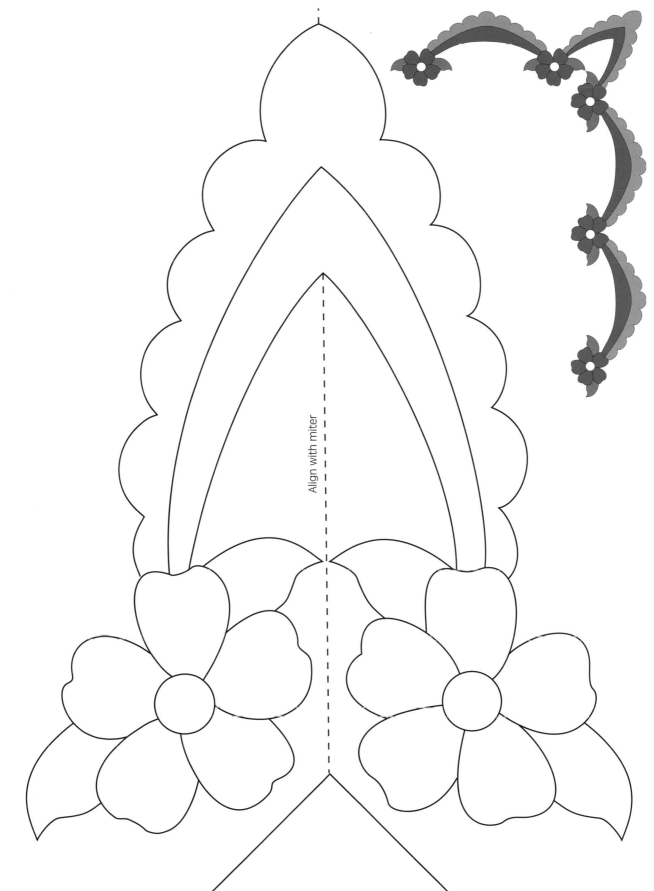

Align with miter

A Baltimore Adventure, Flora and Fauna

A Baltimore Adventure, Flora and Fauna by Ruth H. McIver, 1995. First place in the Amateur Appliqué category at the 1996 AQS Quilt Show. This quilt border was inspired by grapevines growing in the maker's yard. Birds were added for interest. Do you see the worm in the robin's mouth? All of the animals and birds in the quilt are ones Ruth enjoys viewing from her windows, yard, and pasture.

Techniques
Hand appliquéd vines, leaves, and
    grapes
Embroidered tendrils

1. The undulation of the curves is determined by the measurement of the sides. After determining the general curves, draw them on freezer paper. See the directions on page 22 for making the border fit your quilt.
2. Trace all sections of the pattern. Make a pattern for your quilt, using paper cut to fit your border. The patterns provided make one-half of a border and must be reversed to complete the other half. To make adjustments for a shorter or longer border, adjust the undulating vine to fit.
3. Use a light box and blue water eraser marker to transfer the design to the fabric. Test any marker on your fabric before using it to make sure it can be washed out.
4. Make continuous bias by using Celtic bias bars, ¹⁄₁₆"-wide bar for small curves and ¼"-wide bar for the larger vines.
5. Appliqué the vines in place, stitching the insides of the curves first, then the outer edges of the curves.

6. Cut out hundreds of circles for the grapes. Make a cardboard template the finished size of the grape. Take small basting stitches around the edge of the fabric circles. Place the grape template on the wrong side of the fabric circle and pull the basting stitches to gather the circle around the template. Press to establish a crease, remove the template, and tighten the basting thread to reform the circle. Press again. The seam allowance creates the impression of a stuffing.

Ruth used several sources for patterns for the center of the quilt. Several block patterns are from books by Elly Sienkiewicz. The Adventure Ship is her rendition of the reproduction at Charlestowne Landing, Charleston, South Carolina. The Tree of Life central idea came from a greeting card. The boy climbing the fence came from a note pad belonging to her husband's aunt when she was a child.

Finishing touches
The sweeping arc in the corners leads the eye around the corner by continuing the design without any interruption.

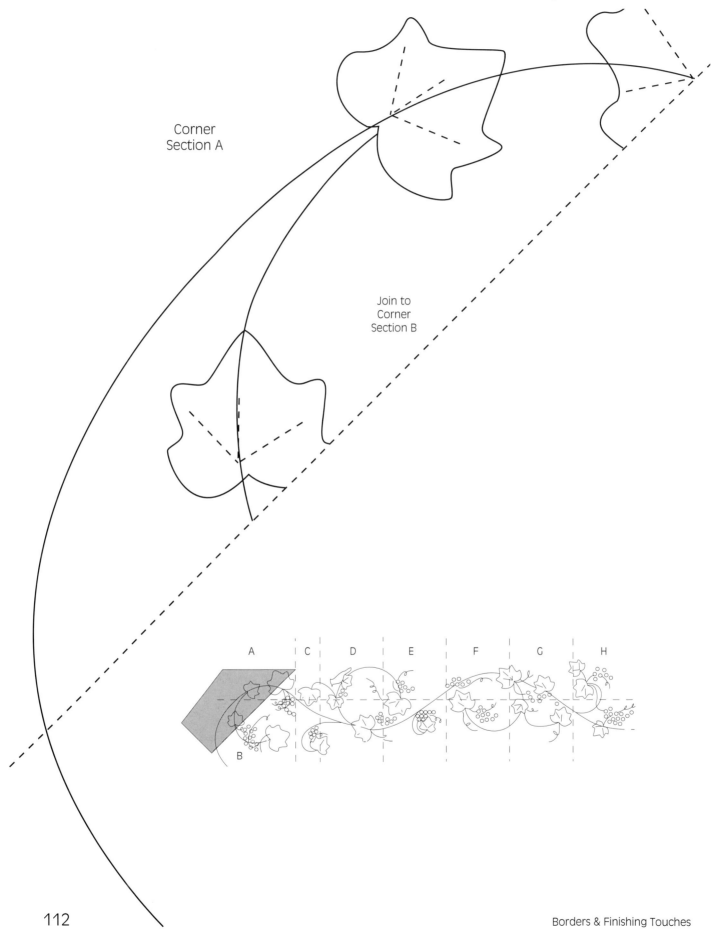

Corner
Section A

Join to
Corner
Section B

A C D E F G H

B

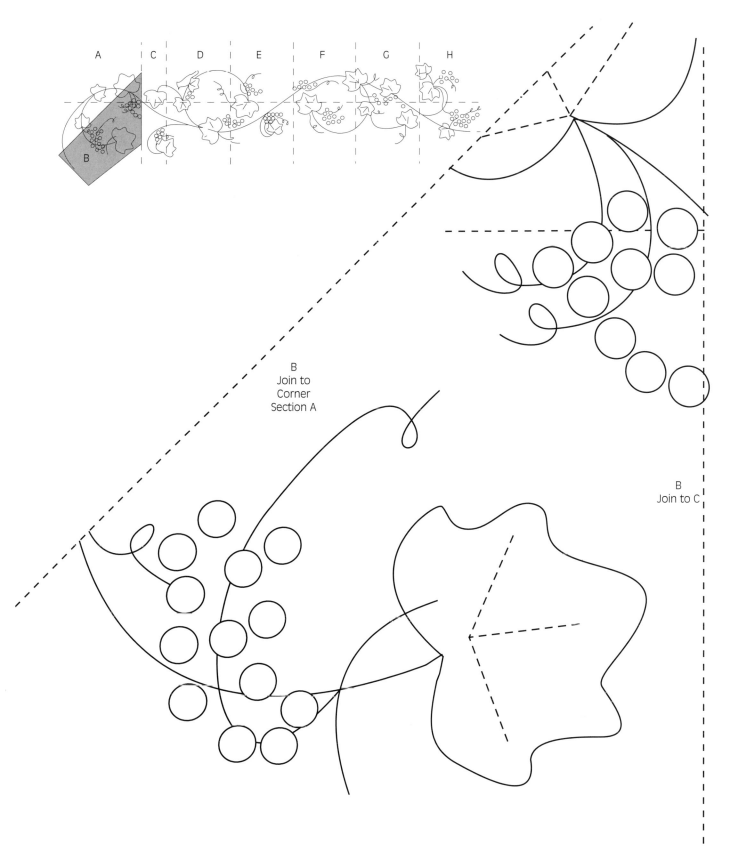

B
Join to
Corner
Section A

B
Join to C

Corner
Section B

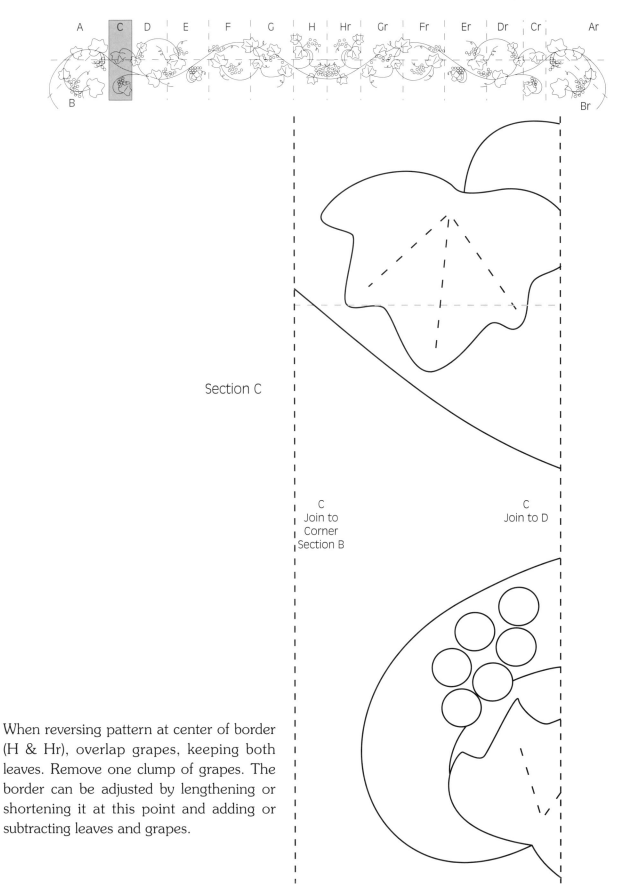

Section C

C
Join to
Corner
Section B

C
Join to D

When reversing pattern at center of border (H & Hr), overlap grapes, keeping both leaves. Remove one clump of grapes. The border can be adjusted by lengthening or shortening it at this point and adding or subtracting leaves and grapes.

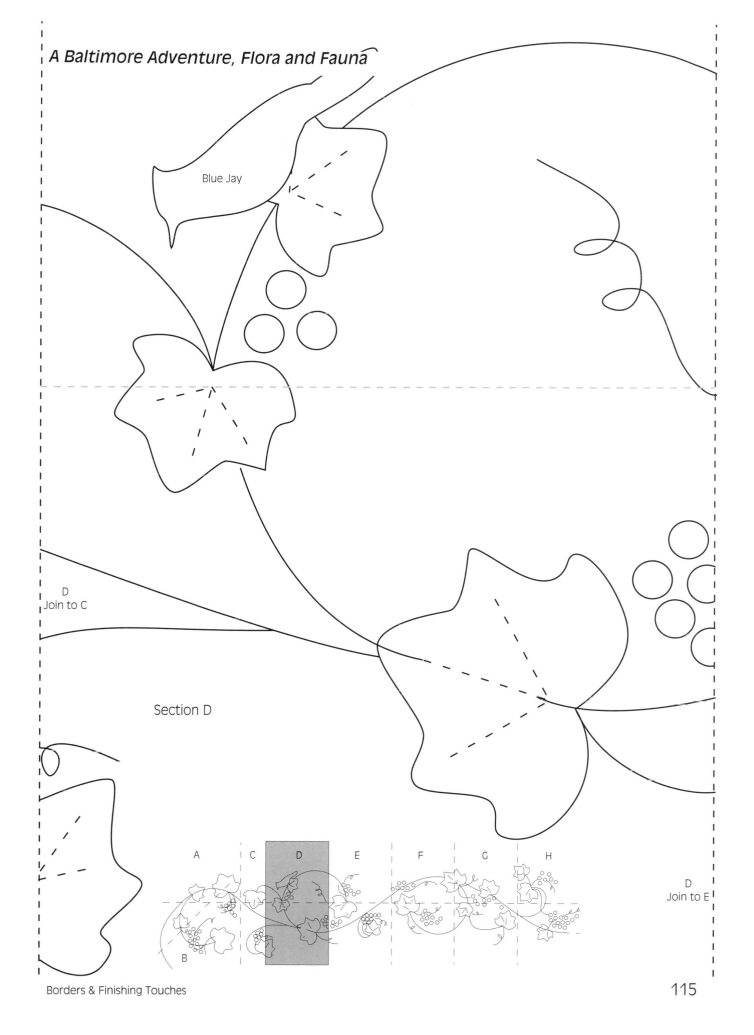

Blue Jay

D
Join to C

Section D

A C D E F G H

B

D
Join to E

Borders & Finishing Touches

G
Join to F

Section G

G
Join to H

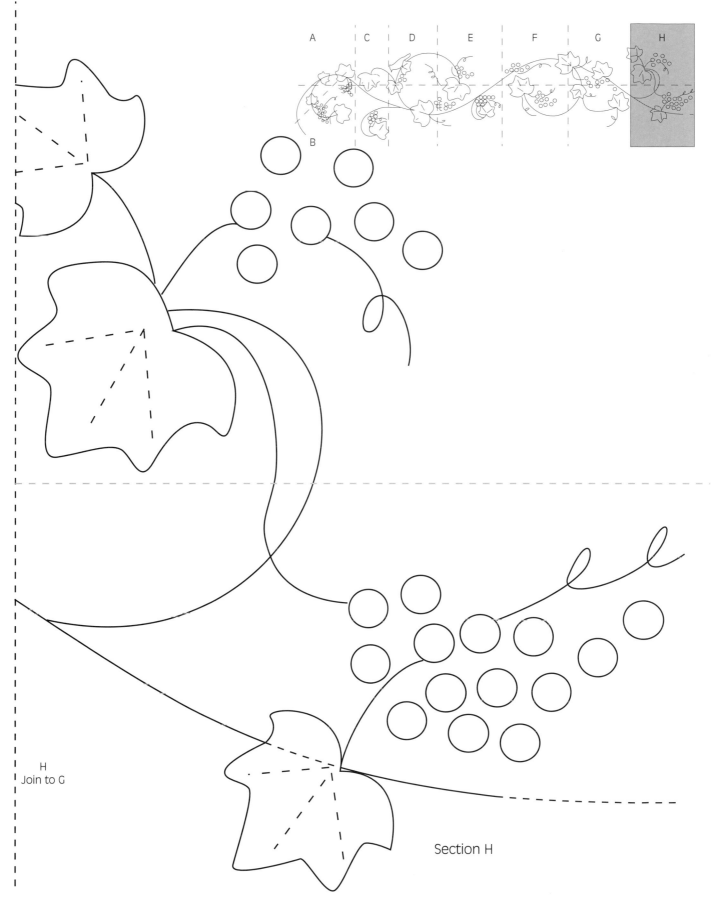

H
Join to G

Section H

The border designs at the beginning of each chapter were designed by the author. These patterns are included so you can try them on one of your quilting projects.

Fern Leaf Swag

Techniques
Appliqué
Reverse appliqué can be used for the vein

1. Make a paper pattern to fit your border following directions on page 22.
2. Draw an undulating line the length of the border.
3. Next, draw the fern pattern with the center of the fern leaf positioned on the arcs of the undulating line.
3. Cut the leaves from one or several fabrics.
4. Appliqué the leaves in place, aligning them with the undulating line.
5. The leaves in the corners have been shortened to fit the space.

Finishing Touches
The center vein can be emphasized by reverse appliquéing a lighter or darker fabric under the opening. Add variety to the design by using several different fabrics. The leaves can be stitched as one piece of fabric. Enhance the vein with embroidery or quilting. This design could be used where a flowing, restful border is needed. It would be especially beautiful with a grid or closely lined background quilting to raise the appliquéd design.

Fern Leaf Swag

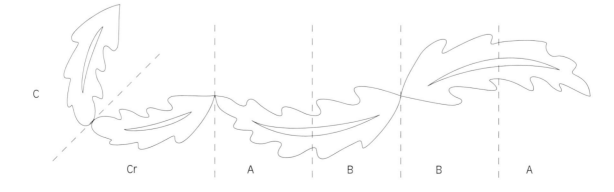

A

Join to B

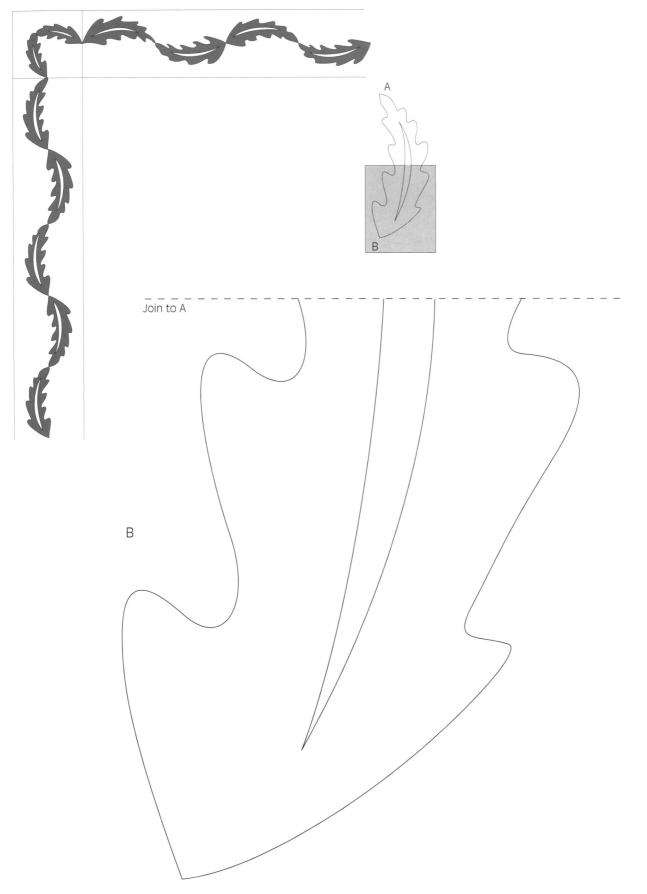

A

B

Join to A

B

Fern Leaf Swag

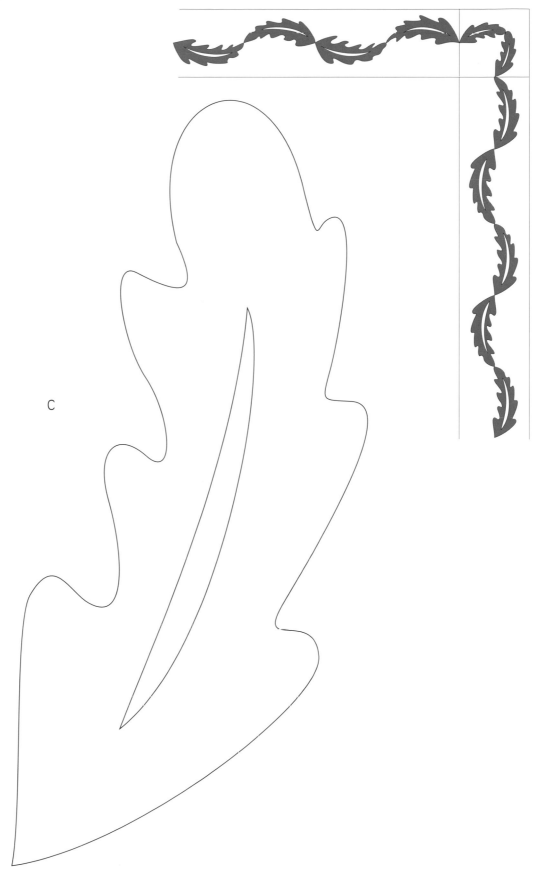

C

Shark's Teeth

Technique
Appliqué

The shark's teeth border can be one of the most versatile styles of borders. It can be used as a single row, multiple rows in different colors, and mirror-imaged rows of teeth can have a narrow or wide strip between the rows. The design shown on page 35 uses mirror-imaged rows of teeth with a band wide enough to stitch a beautiful quilting design in between.

The shark's teeth are scaled so the finished height of the teeth are half the width of the base. For instance, if you want the teeth to be 1" high, the base will be 2". If your quilt is 75" along one side, this example will show you the options available.

75 ÷ 1½" base = 50 teeth ¾" high
75 ÷ 2" base = 37½ teeth 1" high
75 ÷ 2½" base = 30 teeth 1¼" high

A large quilt could support larger teeth, so you might want to use the 2½" base for a quilt this size. Large teeth would probably look out of proportion on a small wallhanging, for which the 1½" base might be a better choice.

1. Cut a center strip of fabric 5½" wide (or the dimension you desire) by the length of the side of your quilt. In this sample, the 5½" width gives a 3"-wide space for quilting between the rows of teeth.

2. The strip of fabric is cut twice the desired height of the teeth plus ½" for seam allowances. If you want to make the teeth 1" high, cut the fabric 2½" wide (2 x 1" + ½") by the length needed.

3. Fold the strip in half, wrong sides together. Baste the strip to the edge of the center strip, with right sides and raw edges together. The folded edge faces the center of the strip. The basting stitches should be ¼" from the raw edge.

4. Starting at one end, measure and mark every 2"; that is the width of the base. Make 1" cuts at these marks, from the folded edge to the basting stitches.

5. To make the teeth, fold the cut edges to form a 45° angle, folding the corners to meet on the back side.

6. Appliqué the edges of the teeth in place. At the inside of the "V," take two or three short stitches to secure the raw edge.

7. Repeat this procedure for the opposite row of teeth. Start marking from the same end as you started marking the first row.

8. The corner can be finished by continuing shark's teeth to the edge, or you can add a triangle across the corner.

9. Binding can be added as usual along the edge, or you might want to wrap the binding completely to the back side of the quilt to let the teeth become the final edge.

Finishing Touches

Multiple rows of shark's teeth can be applied. Several rows can be made from the same piece of fabric by stitching the folds in place. The rows can be staggered. Add variety by using more than one color of fabric.

The teeth can be staggered, as shown in the border on the corner of this page, or spaced evenly on both sides as shown below.

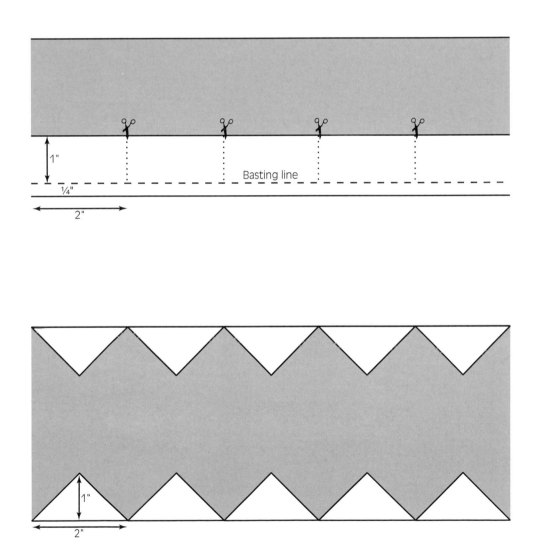

Bibliography

Bacon, Lenice Ingram. *American Patchwork Quilts*, William Morrow & Company Inc., New York, NY, 1973.

Christie, Archibald H. *Pattern Design: An Introduction to the Study of Formal Ornament*, Dover Publications, Inc., New York, NY, 1969.

Hassel, Carla J. *Super Quilter II*, Wallace-Homestead Book Company, Des Moines, IA, 1982.

Hinson, Delores A. *Quilting Manual: New Designer's Boutique*, Hearthside Press Inc., New York, NY, 1970.

James, Michael. *The Quiltmaker's Handbook: A Guide to Design and Construction*, Prentice-Hall, Inc., Englewood Cliffs, NJ, 1978.

Marston, Gwen and Joe Cunningham. *Sets & Borders*, American Quilter's Society, Paducah, KY, 1987.

Martin, Judy and Marsha McCloskey. *Pieced Borders: The Complete Resource*, Crosley-Griffith Publishing Company, Inc., Grinnell, IA, 1994.

Meyer, Franz Sales. *Handbook of Ornament*, Dover Publications, Inc., New York, NY, 1957.

Miller, Phyllis D. *Encyclopedia of Designs for Quilting*, American Quilter's Society, Paducah, KY, 1996.

Morris, Patricia J. *The Judge's Task: How Award-Winning Quilts Are Selected*, American Quilter's Society, Paducah, KY, 1993.

Petrie, W.M. Flinders. *Decorative Symbols and Motifs for Artists and Craftspeople*, Dover Publications, Inc., New York, NY, 1986.

Safford, Carleton L. and Robert Bishop. *America's Quilts & Coverlets*, E. P. Dutton & Co., Inc., New York, NY, 1972.

Speltz, Alexander. *The Styles of Ornament*, Dover Publications, Inc., New York, NY, 1959.

About the Author

Bonnie learned to sew in a very traditional way — her mother taught her. Those first experiences of sitting at the treadle sewing machine served her well, leading the way to a lifetime of enjoyment from working with her hands. Sewing and other forms of needlework may have been the beginning, but Bonnie also enjoys drawing and painting, both in watercolors and oils.

It was while taking a college art course in the 1970s that she made her first quilt. Weather vanes were drawn and silk screened onto muslin for a class assignment; they were sewn together with sashing and a border, and hand quilted. The next quilt was a sampler style that, to this day, has not been quilted. It was a learning tool and Bonnie learned that she most enjoyed the design phase of quiltmaking.

Teaching seemed a natural for this avid needle artist, and it was a great way to share her knowledge in pattern design, counted cross stitch, and quilting. In 1986, Bonnie was certified as a quilt judge by the National Quilting Association. Later, she qualified to judge master quilts as well. Today, while employed at the American Quilter's Society in Paducah, Kentucky, Bonnie still finds time to do some traveling both across the United States and abroad to judge quilt shows and teach quiltmaking. Even though she coordinates one of the largest quilt shows in the country, some of her free time is used to design and make quilts. She continues to enter competitions, and has won numerous awards at regional and national quilt shows.

Writing and editing books is another way Bonnie shares her quilting knowledge. She wrote *Ribbons & Threads: Baltimore Style*, AQS, 1996; and edited *Who's Who in American Quilting*, AQS, 1996; and *A Quilted Christmas*, AQS, 1995.

Do all the good you can,
In all the ways you can,
To all the souls you can,
In all the places you can,
At all the times you can,
With all the zeal you can,
As long as ever you can.

John Wesley
"Rule," late 18th century

AQS Books on Quilts

This is only a partial listing of the books on quilts that are available from the American Quilter's Society. AQS books are known the world over for their timely topics, clear writing, beautiful color photographs, and accurate illustrations and patterns. The following books are available from your local bookseller, quilt shop, or public library. If you are unable to locate certain titles in your area, you may order by mail from the AMERICAN QUILTER'S SOCIETY, P.O. Box 3290, Paducah, KY 42002-3290. Add $2.00 for postage for the first book ordered and 40¢ for each additional book. Include item number, title, and price when ordering. Allow 14 to 21 days for delivery. Customers with Visa, MasterCard, or Discover may phone in orders from 7:00–5:00 CST, Monday–Friday, Toll Free 1-800-626-5420.

4595	**Above & Beyond Basics,** Karen Kay Buckley	$18.95
2282	**Adapting Architectural Details for Quilts,** Carol Wagner	$12.95
4813	**Addresses & Birthdays,** compiled by Klaudeen Hansen **(HB)**	$14.95
4543	**American Quilt Blocks: 50 Patterns for 50 States,** Beth Summers	$16.95
4696	**Amish Kinder Komforts,** Bettina Havig	$14.95
4829	**Anita Shackelford: Surface Textures,** Anita Shackelford **(HB)**	$24.95
4899	**Appliqué Paper Greetings,** Elly Sienkiewicz **(HB)**	$24.95
3790	**Appliqué Patterns from Native American Beadwork Designs,** Dr. Joyce Mori	$14.95
2099	**Ask Helen: More About Quilting Designs,** Helen Squire	$14.95
2207	**Award-Winning Quilts: 1985-1987**	$24.95
2354	**Award-Winning Quilts: 1988-1989**	$24.95
3425	**Award-Winning Quilts: 1990-1991**	$24.95
3791	**Award-Winning Quilts: 1992-1993**	$24.95
4830	**Baskets: Celtic Style,** Scarlett Rose	$19.95
4832	**A Batch of Patchwork,** May T. Miller & Susan B. Burton	$18.95
4593	**Blossoms by the Sea: Making Ribbon Flowers for Quilts,** Faye Labanaris	$24.95
4898	**Borders & Finishing Touches,** Bonnie K. Browning	$16.95
4697	**Caryl Bryer Fallert: A Spectrum of Quilts, 1983-1995,** Caryl Bryer Fallert	$24.95
4626	**Celtic Geometric Quilts,** Camille Remme	$16.95
3926	**Celtic Style Floral Appliqué,** Scarlett Rose	$14.95
2208	**Classic Basket Quilts,** Elizabeth Porter & Marianne Fons	$16.95
2355	**Creative Machine Art,** Sharee Dawn Roberts	$24.95
4818	**Dear Helen, Can You Tell Me?** Helen Squire	$15.95
3399	**Dye Painting!** Ann Johnston	$19.95
4814	**Encyclopedia of Designs for Quilting,** Phyllis D. Miller **(HB)**	$34.95
3468	**Encyclopedia of Pieced Quilt Patterns,** compiled by Barbara Brackman	$34.95
3846	**Fabric Postcards,** Judi Warren	$22.95
4594	**Firm Foundations,** Jane Hall & Dixie Haywood	$18.95
4900	**Four Blocks Continued...,** Linda Giesler Carlson	$16.95
2381	**From Basics to Binding,** Karen Kay Buckley	$16.95
4526	**Gatherings: America's Quilt Heritage,** Kathlyn F. Sullivan	$34.95
2097	**Heirloom Miniatures,** Tina M. Gravatt	$9.95
4628	**Helen's Guide to quilting in the 21st century,** Helen Squire	$16.95
1906	**Irish Chain Quilts: A Workbook of Irish Chains,** Joyce B. Peaden	$14.95
3784	**Jacobean Appliqué: Book I, "Exotica,"** Campbell & Ayars	$18.95
4544	**Jacobean Appliqué: Book II, "Romantica,"** Campbell & Ayars	$18.95
3904	**The Judge's Task,** Patricia J. Morris	$19.95
4751	**Liberated Quiltmaking,** Gwen Marston **(HB)**	$24.95
4897	**Lois Smith's Machine Quiltmaking,** Lois Smith	$19.95
4523	**Log Cabin Quilts: New Quilts from an Old Favorite**	$14.95
4545	**Log Cabin with a Twist,** Barbara T. Kaempfer	$18.95
4815	*Love to Quilt:* **Bears, Bears, Bears,** Karen Kay Buckley	$14.95
4833	*Love to Quilt:* **Broderie Perse: The Elegant Quilt,** Barbara W. Barber	$14.95
4598	*Love to Quilt:* **Men's Vests,** Alexandra Capadalis Dupré	$14.95
4816	*Love to Quilt:* **Necktie Sampler Blocks,** Janet B. Elwin	$14.95
4753	*Love to Quilt:* **Penny Squares,** Willa Baranowski	$12.95
4911	**Mariner's Compass Quilts: New Quilts from an Old Favorite**	$16.95
4752	**Miniature Quilts: Connecting New & Old Worlds,** Tina M. Gravatt	$14.95
4514	**Mola Techniques for Today's Quilters,** Charlotte Patera	$18.95
3330	**More Projects and Patterns,** Judy Florence	$18.95
1981	**Nancy Crow: Quilts and Influences,** Nancy Crow	$29.95
3331	**Nancy Crow: Work in Transition,** Nancy Crow	$12.95
4828	**Nature, Design & Silk Ribbons,** Cathy Grafton	$18.95
3332	**New Jersey Quilts,**The Heritage Quilt Project of New Jersey	$29.95
3927	**New Patterns from Old Architecture,** Carol Wagner	$12.95
2153	**No Dragons on My Quilt,** Jean Ray Laury	$12.95
4627	**Ohio Star Quilts: New Quilts from an Old Favorite**	$16.95
3469	**Old Favorites in Miniature,** Tina Gravatt	$15.95
4831	**Optical Illusions for Quilters,** Karen Combs	$22.95
4515	**Paint and Patches: Painting on Fabrics with Pigment,** Vicki L. Johnson	$18.95
4513	**Plaited Patchwork,** Shari Cole	$19.95
3928	**Precision Patchwork for Scrap Quilts,** Jeannette Tousley Muir	$12.95
4779	**Protecting Your Quilts: A Guide for Quilt Owners, Second Edition**	$6.95
4542	**A Quilted Christmas,** edited by Bonnie Browning	$18.95
2380	**Quilter's Registry,** Lynne Fritz	$9.95
3467	**Quilting Patterns from Native American Designs,** Dr. Joyce Mori	$12.95
3470	**Quilting with Style,** Gwen Marston & Joe Cunningham	$24.95
2284	**Quiltmaker's Guide: Basics & Beyond,** Carol Doak	$19.95
4918	**Quilts by Paul D. Pilgrim: Blending the Old & the New,** Gerald E. Roy	$16.95
2257	*Quilts:* **The Permanent Collection – MAQS**	$9.95
3793	*Quilts:* **The Permanent Collection – MAQS Volume II**	$9.95
3789	**Roots, Feathers & Blooms,** Linda Giesler Carlson	$16.95
4512	**Sampler Quilt Blocks from Native American Designs,** Dr. Joyce Mori	$14.95
3796	**Seasons of the Heart & Home: Quilts for a Winter's Day,** Jan Patek	$18.95
3761	**Seasons of the Heart & Home: Quilts for Summer Days,** Jan Patek	$18.95
2357	**Sensational Scrap Quilts,** Darra Duffy Williamson	$24.95
4783	**Silk Ribbons by Machine,** Jeanie Sexton	$15.95
3929	**The Stori Book of Embellishing,** Mary Stori	$16.95
3903	**Straight Stitch Machine Appliqué,** Letty Martin	$16.95
3792	**Striplate Piecing,** Debra Wagner	$24.95
3930	**Tessellations & Variations,** Barbara Ann Caron	$14.95
3788	**Three-Dimensional Appliqué,** Anita Shackelford	$24.95
4596	**Ties, Ties, Ties: Traditional Quilts from Neckties,** Janet B. Elwin	$19.95
3931	**Time-Span Quilts: New Quilts from Old Tops,** Becky Herdle	$16.95
4919	**Transforming Fabric,** Carolyn Dahl	$29.95
2029	**A Treasury of Quilting Designs,** Linda Goodmon Emery	$14.95
3847	**Tricks with Chintz,** Nancy S. Breland	$14.95
2286	**Wonderful Wearables: A Celebration of Creative Clothing,** Virginia Avery	$24.95
4812	**Who's Who in American Quilting,** edited by Bonnie Browning **(HB)**	$49.95
4956	**Variegreat! New Dimensions in Traditional Quilts,** Linda Glantz	$19.95
4972	**20th Century Quilts,** Cuesta Benberry and Joyce Gross	$ 9.95